DECIPHERING THE LEARNING DOMAINS:

A Second Generation Classification Model for Educational Objectives

Walter D. Pierce
Charles E. Gray
Illinois State University

University Press
of America™

370.1523
P61d
118819
July 1981

PREFACE

The typical classroom teacher on occasion finds frustration in his daily endeavors when the realization occurs that there must be more to learning than the rote memorization of facts or the understanding of concepts. The mind and body is capable of so much more, and most educators intuitively feel this and yearn to assist youngsters to expand and grow beyond the expectation usually dictated by the traditional educational pattern.

It is the intention of this book to provide a model that will assist the pre-service or practicing teacher to envision a variety of levels in the cognitive, affective, and psychomotor domains and to strive to provide student learning experiences throughout all levels of all domains.

* * * * *

In producing this volume, the authors would like to express their appreciation to Alberta Carr for her help in preparing the book to go to press. In addition, the work of Albert Upton, J. P. Guilford, Benjamin Bloom, David Krathwohl, Lawrence Metcalf, Lawrence Kohlberg, and A. Dean Hauenstein must be acknowledged as fundamental to the conceptualization of the classification model presented herein.

W.D.P./C.E.G.

TABLE OF CONTENTS

Page

PREFACE   i

CHAPTER

I. TEACHING IN THE THREE DOMAINS:
    IMBALANCE, AMBIGUITY, AND FRUSTRATION . .   1

        Educational Objectives and
            the Three Domains   1

        Traditional Emphasis of
            the Cognitive Domain   3

        Vagueness of the
            Affective Domain   6

        Second-class Citizen Status
            of the Psychomotor Domain   8

        Assumptions About
            Educational Objectives   9

        The Plan of the Book   10

        Endnotes   11

II. INTELLECTUAL ENDEAVORS:
    THE KING OF THE DOMAINS   13

        Historical Development
            of the Cognitive Domain   13

        Possible Classification Schemes
            for Objectives   15

            Upton's "Design for Thinking" . .   15
            Guilford's "Structure of
                Intellect"   16

Gagné's Analysis
   of Instructional Objectives . .   18
Bloom's Taxonomy
   of Educational Objectives . . .   20
Summary   20

The Pierce-Gray Classification
Model for the Cognitive Domain . .   21

Level I: Cognitive Perceiving . .   21
Level II: Understanding   24
Level III: Applying   25
Level IV: Analyzing   26
Level V: Cognitive Judging . . .   27
Level VI: Cognitive Creating . .   29

Concluding Remarks   30

Summary of Levels
in the Cognitive Domain   30

Endnotes   31

III. AFFECTIVE ENDEAVORS:
THE QUEEN OF THE DOMAINS   33

The Affective Domain
in Historical Perspective   33

Affective Development and Conflict .   35

Alternative Classification Schemes .   36

Guilford: Structure
   of Intellect   37
Raths: Process of Valuing   37
Maslow: Hierarchy
   of the Needs of Man   39
Broudy: Intrinsic
   and Instrumental Valuing . . .   41
Krathwohl: Affective Domain
   Taxonomy   42

Conclusions About Approaches
to the Affective Domain   44

The Pierce-Gray Classification
Model for the Affective Domain . .   45

The Need for an Effective
Affective Classification
Model   45
Relationship of Affective
and Cognitive Domains   47
Level I: Affective Perceiving . .   48
Level II: Reacting   49
Level III: Conforming   52
Level IV: Validating   53
Level V: Affective Judging . . .   55
Level VI: Affective Creating . .   56

Summary of Levels in
the Affective Domain   59

Endnotes   60

IV.   PHYSICAL ENDEAVORS:
THE PRINCE OF THE DOMAINS   63

A Review of Psychomotor
Classifications   63

Ragsdale   63
Simpson   64
Kibler, Barker, and Miles   64
Hauenstein   64
Harrow   65

Conclusions Regarding Psychomotor
Classification Schemes   66

The Pierce-Gray Classification
Model for the Psychomotor Domain .   66

Level I: Psychomotor Perceiving .   67
Level II: Activating   68
Level III: Executing   70
Level IV: Maneuvering   71
Level V: Psychomotor Judging . .   72
Level VI: Psychomotor Creating .   73

Summary of Levels in the
Psychomotor Domain   74

Endnotes   75

V.   STRATEGIES IN THE USE
     OF THE COGNITIVE DOMAIN   77

        Correspondence between Objectives,
           Learning Activities,
           and Evaluations   77

        Ensuring a Cross-section
           of Intellectual Endeavors   79

        Using the Classification
           Model in Planning   80

        Cognitive Levels Used in
           Selecting Teaching Strategies . .   84

           Exposition   84
           Self-instructional Materials . . .   86
           Interaction Techniques   88
           Inquiry Learning   90
           Discussions   94

        Strategies to Inspire
           Cognitive Creating   94

           Teacher Guidelines
              to Stimulate Creativity   96

        Conclusion   98

        Endnotes   98

VI. STRATEGIES IN THE USE
     OF THE AFFECTIVE DOMAIN 101

        Defining Affective Behavior,
           Goals, and Teacher Role 101

           Affects 101
           Attitudes and Values 102
           General Affective Goals 103
           Rationale for Teacher Role 104

        Relationship between Objectives,
           Learning Activities,
           and Evaluations 105

Using the Affective Classification
Model in Planning   108

Guidelines for Affective
Perceiving Objectives   109
Guidelines for Reacting
Objectives   109
Guidelines for
Conforming Objectives   110
Guidelines for
Validating Objectives   110
Guidelines for Affective
Judging Objectives   111
Guidelines for Affective
Creating Objectives   111

Classification of Affective
Teaching Strategies   117

Types of Affective
Teaching Strategies   117
Value Clarification   117
Value Analysis   117
Moral Reasoning   118

Descriptions of Affective
Teaching Strategies   118

Value Clarification
Strategies   118
Value Analysis Strategies . . .   138
Moral Reasoning Strategies . . .   147

Strategies for Activating
the Creative Imagination   158

Endnotes   160

VII. STRATEGIES IN THE USE
OF THE PSYCHOMOTOR DOMAIN   165

Objective, Activity, and
Evaluation Correspondence   165

Neglect of Higher
Psychomotor Levels   166

Using the Psychomotor
    Classification Model
    in Planning 167

Psychomotor Levels and Strategies . . 167

    Psychomotor Perceiving-
        Activating 168
    Deliberate Modeling 172
    Executing 173
    Maneuvering 176
    Psychomotor Judging 178
    Psychomotor Creating 178

    Endnotes 181

VIII. VIEWING THE THREE DOMAINS 183

    The Domain CAP 183

    Relationships between the Domains . . 185

        Level I: Cognitive Perceiving-
            Affective Perceiving-
            Psychomotor Perceiving 185
        Level II: Understanding-
            Reacting-Activating 186
        Level III: Applying-
            Conforming-Executing 186
        Level IV: Analyzing-
            Validating-Maneuvering 187
        Level V: Cognitive-Affective-
            Psychomotor Judging 187
        Level VI: Cognitive-Affective-
            Psychomotor Creating 187

    Achieving Domain Balance 188

        Struggles for Domain Dominance . . 188
        Shifts in Domain Emphasis 190
        Domain Emphasis in the Schools . . 193
        The Goal-oriented, Domain-
            balanced Secondary School . . . 193

    The Right and Left Hemispheres
        of the Brain and the
        Three Domains 196

Page

Endnotes 196

APPENDICES

    A--Pierce-Gray Classification Model for
    the Cognitive, Affective, and
    Psychomotor Domain (Summary Outline) . . 201

    B--Model for the Analysis and Comparison
    of Cultural Value Systems
    (With Probing Questions) 203

    C--Heuristic Evaluative Model (Analysis
    and Testing of Value Judgments) 209

    D--Development of Moral Judgment
    (Or Reasoning) 221

    E--Methods and Educational Programs for
    Stimulating Creativity:
    A Representative List 235

INDEX 241

CHAPTER I--Teaching in the Three Domains:
Imbalance, Ambiguity, and Frustration

EDUCATIONAL OBJECTIVES AND
THE THREE DOMAINS

Today most educators would agree that instructional planning and assessment is more effective when teachers and students are clear about the objectives they hope to achieve. A concomitant problem, however, is that insignificant objectives take less effort to make clear and, in turn, are easily developed and assessed. The result may be learning that is of little consequence in terms of the array of knowledge and skills peculiar to a field of study, or of little meaning in relation to the needs of learners. One procedure for avoiding this phenomenon is the use of a comprehensive approach for identifying basic objectives, along with a workable system of categorizing objectives into areas or levels. Such classification systems help to ensure a balance in pupil educational development, and provide a framework that can be used by teachers as a guide in developing specific instructional objectives appropriate for students in given instructional settings.

Historically, there have been many efforts to identify broad objectives for public education. Work by the Committee of Ten in 1893,[1] The Committee on College Entrance Requirements in 1899,[2] The Commission on the Reorganization of Secondary Education in 1918,[3] The American Youth Commission in 1937,[4] The Educational Policies Commission in 1938,[5] The National Association of Secondary School Principals in 1947,[6] and the Educational Policies Commission in 1961[7] were all attempts to identify the then prevailing purposes

1

of public education. These efforts were worthwhile, but failed to supply the practicing teacher with conceptual models that can be used to translate broad goals into manageable instructional objectives.

Over the centuries, man has attempted to classify human behavior in various ways. Many such classification schemes can be traced back to Aristotle's analysis of the nature of man. Aristotle maintained that human beings were subject to a growth impulse that was expressed through three forms, or souls. The nutritive (or vegetative) form was said to control vegetative and reproductive functions; the sensitive (or animal) form controlled functions represented by imagination, perception, memory, pleasure-pain experiences, wishes, and aversions; and the rational (or intellectual) form controlled the functions of concept formation and reasoning.[8] Thus, Aristotle's formulation categorized the functions of thought, emotion, and reproduction. At the dawn of the scientific era, Descartes developed a theory based upon the idea of a dualism between the functions of the mind (soul) and the body (matter). For him, the qualities of willing, imagining, desiring, thinking, hoping, doubting, perceiving, and so forth, were all modes of two basic mental powers; the power of understanding (or the intellect), and the power of will (or volition). The operation of the understanding and the will were distinct from the body, which operated in accordance with mechanistic (or involuntary) principles. Descartes also classified the basic unlearned human emotions into the six categories of wonder, love, hatred, desire, joy, and sorrow.[9] Later efforts by empirical philosophers to resolve the problems inherent in Descartes' dualism of mind and body eventually stimulated the beginnings of modern psychology.

In the twentieth century, several scholars have explored the nature of the intellect and consequently a number of useful models have been developed. For example, Thorndike identified what he termed the three constellations of abilities which were labeled the linguistic, the mechanical, and the social. Guilford identified the mental operations of cognition, memory, divergent production, convergent production, and evaluation, which the human organism utilizes in dealing with four distinct types of content (figural, symbolic, semantic, and behavioral).[10] However, the more comprehensive formulations of Upton[11] and Bloom, et al.,[12] are likely to be of more immediate value to educators

concerned with categorizing educational objectives.
Upton and Bloom tend to parallel each other in the
sense that they both classify human behavior into
categories of intellectual, emotional, and physical
endeavors. Upton labeled his categories logical, affective, and sensory. Bloom, et al., labeled theirs
the cognitive, affective, and psychomotor domains.

At present, the last three categories seem to hold
the most promise for education. The Bloom models (or
taxonomies) have been widely accepted and used in
teacher education programs and school systems and by
state departments of education and educational researchers. In fact, today, when practitioners speak
of classification systems for educational objectives,
they are usually referring to the three domains and
allude to the work of Bloom. Use of the category systems presented in the taxonomies has prompted educators to think more carefully and precisely about what
they intend to accomplish in given curricular programs,
courses, or units of study. The intention of this
book is not to depreciate the taxonomies or the contri-
butions they have made in moving curriculum planners
and teachers toward improved planning and precision
with regard to educational outcomes. However, there
are a number of problems related to the design and
application of the taxonomic classification systems as
they are presently formulated. Several of these problems will be delineated in the following sections.

TRADITIONAL EMPHASIS OF THE COGNITIVE DOMAIN

Traditionally, the concept cognitive abilities
has been used to include all of the intellectual abilities (i.e., all types of thinking or uses of intelligence). However, a degree of confusion has accompanied
the use of the above terms because of the different
ways in which they have been employed by scholars.
For example, Bloom's cognitive taxonomy includes the
categories of Knowledge, Comprehension, Application,
Analysis, Synthesis, and Evaluation, but he refers to
only the last five as Intellectual Abilities and
Skills. Upton's model employs the rubric logical for
the cognitive skills of qualification, operational
analysis, classification, and structural analysis. On
the other hand, Guilford's Structure of Intellect model
includes 120 Intellectual Abilities that involve the
mental operations of Cognition, Memory, Divergent

3

Production, Convergent Production, and Evaluation.[13]
For the purposes of this book we will use the term
cognitive to refer to all of the intellectual processes
of Bloom, Upton, and Guilford, although from time to
time it will be helpful to distinguish between the
higher and lower cognitive abilities in the following
manner:

>Lower Cognitive Abilities: perceiving,
>storing, and retrieving information, or
>cognitive-memory abilities (Bloom:
>Knowledge; Upton: Qualification; and
>Guilford: Cognition and Memory).

>Higher Cognitive Abilities: organizing
>and using information in the solving of
>problems, or critical and reflective
>thinking (Bloom: all levels above Knowl-
>edge; Upton: Classification, Operational
>Analysis, and Structural Analysis; and
>Guilford: all operations except Cognition
>and Memory).

Examinations of textbooks, instructional tapes,
films, and frequent classroom observations lead one
inevitably to the conclusion that schools place considerable emphasis on learning in the cognitive domain.
For years, methods course instructors, school supervisors, professional organizations, and educational
commentators and writers have noted, documented, and
often deplored the fact that most schools devote a dis-
proportionate amount of time to activities designed to
promote cognitive learning (at the expense of affective
and psychomotor learning, and in spite of goals to the
contrary contained in curriculum guides). Many ob-
servers maintain, further, that higher level cognitive
learning is neglected in the schools. Learning at the
memory level is emphasized and consequently students
are seldom engaged in learning activities at or above
an understanding level.

Many factors help to explain the apparent popular-
ity of cognitive learning in the schools. Teachers,
like anyone else, tend to internalize the models they
have encountered in their own formative years. Hence,
many teachers almost unconsciously imitate the modes
of teaching they observed during their own school and
college days. Many professors, even those in colleges
of education, continue to teach in a manner that implies that cognitive learning is the only kind of
learning that is really worthwhile and respectable.

It is also quite true that in certain respects it is easier to plan and implement cognitive learning activities than activities in the other domains; and certainly much less effort is required in working toward lower-level cognitive objectives than is the case with higher-level objectives. For example, it is much easier to plan a lesson where students are to memorize or summarize materials than it is to plan lessons that would involve practical applications, serious evaluation, or the exploration and clarification of value positions relative to the material.

A case can be made that there is often a potential "danger" for the teacher when his students begin to operate at higher cognitive levels or when they become involved in activities with strong affective overtones. As soon as students move away from mere learning of what is presented to them, they often may become somewhat critical of what they encounter. They may pose difficult questions or inquire into issues that embarrass, confound, or disturb their elders. The adult world does not take well to "smart-aleck kids" who interpret things in "different" ways, come up with new or novel conclusions, ponder the validity of the values they have been taught to accept without question, or wish to engage in unconventional physical activities. Thus, many teachers may very well feel they are asking for trouble if they try to involve students in thinking at the higher cognitive levels or in activities related to the psychomotor or affective domains (and teachers are often quite correct in sensing such potential difficulties).

Learning beyond the cognitive domain is also inhibited by some teachers who lack a comprehensive view of the methodology, goals, and findings of their teaching area, and hence fail to perceive the possibility of psychomotor, affective, or higher-level cognitive objectives that might be related to their field. Often teachers view their subject field as a body of data to be mastered, and simply do not perceive of any way in which the content can be related to a broad range of instructional objectives.

Finally, it is important to realize that many pupils tend to resist attempts to involve them in unfamiliar learning patterns; they may feel reasonably comfortable with the learning modes to which they are accustomed and confident of their ability to adjust or achieve within the confines of the traditional pattern (this is quite often true of high-ability students).

Many students find that "thinking" at the higher cognitive levels is just a lot of hard work. Others view "affective" involvement as similar to bull-sessions and although sometimes fun and interesting, it isn't really important as part of their course work. Still others have been taught that the development of psychomotor skills is only for those of inferior cognitive ability.

Thus it is clear that there are roadblocks which influence the teacher to operate primarily within the lower levels of the cognitive domain. What practicing teachers need is a comprehensive model or approach that will enable them to relate the domains to each other in a practical way, and make it relatively easy for them to see how a wide range of objectives could be related to both a teaching field and students.

VAGUENESS OF THE AFFECTIVE DOMAIN

An examination of school statements of philosophy or departmental or course objectives reveals an apparent concern about learning and behavior in the affective domain. However, once one begins to probe for the meanings and implications of the statements of philosophy and intent, problems emerge. First, there often seems to be considerable ambiguity (and little agreement) as to what is meant by affective learning. Second, actual classroom practice often appears to have only a minimal relationship to stated affective objectives. And third, there is considerable confusion and inconsistency regarding the types of teaching strategies (and content) that might be appropriate for promoting affective learning.

For example, one teacher might regard affective education as a means of assisting students in developing viable and consistent self concepts. But another teacher in the same school might consider student acceptance of traditional cultural values as the prime concern in the affective domain. A third teacher might wish his students to search out (or develop) universal principles that could serve as goals for the shaping of a more just and humane social order. Other teachers might be categorized as eclectics and adopt elements from several of the positions described above. When translated into educational practice, such a variety of viewpoints results in the pedagogical potpourri that goes under the rubrics of affective learning, values education, character development, or cultural

6

socialization.

No matter what the school or teacher goals might be, the way in which they are implemented in the classroom may very well negate or subvert the original objectives--or have no relation to them whatsoever. For instance, the teacher who wishes students to improve their self concepts might very well be defeating the purpose by attempting to force teacher perceptions and values on the students. Or the teacher who wants students to make up their own minds about certain issues might actually be indoctrinating them by the way in which the issues under consideration are approached.

A definite "vagueness" and logical inconsistency frequently accompanies discussions related to the affective domain. Affective behaviors are thought of as "feelings," "attitudes," and "values," consequently it is difficult to operationalize and measure such entities. Some have said that affects cannot be dealt with cognitively, while others maintain that cognitive skills can be employed to analyze and change affective dispositions. Some teachers are very much interested in changing the attitudes and values of their students, while other teachers feel they should not in any way tamper with student beliefs. Terms commonly employed in the affective realm are poorly defined, and hence carry a variety of meanings; classification schemes lack precision and fail to discriminate between different levels of intensity of "feeling." The relationship between the process of cognitive evaluation and the affective domain is not clearly spelled out. Such confusions often lead teachers to deal with values (and affects) when they do not intend to do so, and conversely to fail to adequately examine values when they in fact wish to do so. It is not uncommon for teachers to take the position that one opinion or belief is as good as another, all in the name of "freedom of speech." Such a position is in essence intellectually contradictory, since it totally ignores the fundamental premise upon which freedom of speech is based, namely, the subjection of beliefs to the test of evidence and experience in the marketplace of ideas.

In an effort to clarify some of the concepts in the affective domain and to provide teachers with a tool for use in developing affective educational objectives, Krathwohl and his associates developed the Taxonomy of Affective Objectives.[14] The taxonomy has been helpful in providing educators with a common vocabulary and with a more precise conceptual focus when dealing with the affective domain. However, the affective taxonomy is actually a value process model, rather than a classification model of affective behavior (or learning). It is incomplete with respect to identifying the types of "affects" one encounters in dealing with human behavior and further, the nature of its relationship to the cognitive and psychomotor domains is unclear. Also, the higher levels of the taxonomy represent complicated psychological internalizations within the individual, and leave the teacher with little to go on with regard to identifying, analyzing, measuring, or changing such psychological states.

In essence, what is needed is a theoretical construct or model which clearly delineates and classifies the various types of observable behavior that have obvious affective overtones (without losing sight of the cognitive and/or psychomotor aspects of the behaviors). Such a model could be used as a guide in viewing the affective domain and in relating it to the cognitive and psychomotor domains; and hence, serve as the basis for developing appropriate objectives, teaching strategies, and assessment procedures related to affective learning. Utilization of such a model would make possible a needed consistency in the design, implementation, and assessment of the affective components of school programs, courses, and units of study.

SECOND-CLASS CITIZEN STATUS
OF THE PSYCHOMOTOR DOMAIN

While the emphasis in formal education has been mainly cognitive and occasionally affective, the psychomotor domain has been largely ignored except in those courses and curricular areas which have been principally concerned with manual skills or bodily coordination (most usually associated with occupational and physical education). For the most part, teachers and curriculum developers have concentrated mainly on the cognitive and/or affective domains, and frequently consider the psychomotor domain as something largely "alien" to what they feel to be the really important—and academic—concerns of education.

Such a state of affairs has resulted in few serious attempts to relate the three domains in educational practice. Hence, there is presently a need to bring the domains together in a theoretical framework that

8

can be utilized by teachers. There have been several attempts to identify levels in the psychomotor domain. However, the systems developed have been difficult for teachers to use because they are internally inconsistent, or because they present either a highly restricted or an overly complex view of the types of behaviors classified as psychomotor. For the most part, there has been little effort to relate these diverse schemes; and other than the fact that a single publisher has produced volumes dealing with all three of the domains, there has been no concerted effort to relate the psychomotor to the other two domains of learning.[15]

ASSUMPTIONS ABOUT EDUCATIONAL OBJECTIVES

As previously stated, it is an assumption of this book that clarity in the statement of instructional objectives is an important prerequisite for effective instructional planning and assessment. A further assumption is that internally consistent and logically related systems for classifying objectives, in terms of the possible range of human cognitive, affective, and psychomotor capabilities, would be appropriate and useful as tools to aid teachers in developing appropriate objectives for their courses and programs of instruction.

The case for how precise objectives should be, or exactly which types of objectives should be developed in a school or course is discussed at length in the educational literature of the various subject areas, and is not the focus of this volume. However, it is the intent herein to state and defend the following propositions:

1. That clearly stated instructional objectives are useful (if not essential) in the planning and assessment of educational programs;

2. That classifying objectives into specific domains in a generally hierarchical and logical order is helpful in the planning and assessment process;

3. That the classification systems should be practical and readily adaptable to the needs of practicing teachers;

9

4. That the classification systems should be (a) internally consistent, and insofar as possible, (b) logically related to each other;

5. That the classification systems (and their posited interrelationships) should be based upon basic theory about the types and range of human cognitive, affective, and psychomotor capabilities.

The formulations, schemes, and relationships presented in this book are an attempt to operationalize the above propositions and assumptions in a way that can be directly applied to the tasks and problems of instructional planning in educational institutions or settings of every type.

THE PLAN OF THE BOOK

This book is divided into eight chapters. Following the present introductory chapter are three chapters, each of which deals with one of the learning domains; the cognitive, affective, and psychomotor domains, respectively. Each domain is discussed in terms of how it has been perceived historically; and in each instance some of the related theory and research is summarized. For each domain, the authors present and describe in detail a new classification system.

The next three chapters are concerned with the practical applications of the new classification systems. A variety of examples and recommended uses of the classification schemes are discussed. Also, teaching strategies appropriate for achieving objectives in each domain are described.

A final chapter attempts an overall conceptualization and synthesis of the three classification models, including a section that discusses the relationships between the three domains. In addition, the chapter suggests ways of achieving domain balance in developing curricular programs. For the convenience of the reader, a brief outline summary of the three classification systems is presented in Appendix A.

ENDNOTES

[1]Committee on Secondary School Studies, _Report of the Committee on Secondary School Studies Appointed at the Meeting of the National Education Association, July 9, 1892_ (Washington, D.C.: Government Printing Office, 1893).

[2]National Education Association, _Report of the Committee on College Entrance Requirements_ (Washington, D.C.: National Education Association, 1899).

[3]_Cardinal Principles of Education_, Bulletin #35 (Washington, D.C.: United States Bureau of Education, 1918), pp. 5-10.

[4]H. R. Douglass, _Secondary Education for Youth in Modern America_ (Washington, D.C.: American Council on Education, 1937), p. 137.

[5]Educational Policies Commission, _The Purpose of Education in American Democracy_ (Washington, D.C.: National Education Association, 1938), pp. 50, 72, 90, 108.

[6]_The Imperative Needs of Youth of Secondary School Age_, Bulletin of National Association of Secondary School Principals, XXXI (Washington, D.C.: National Education Association, March, 1947).

[7]_The Central Purpose of American Education_ (Washington, D.C.: National Education Association, 1961).

[8]Carlton H. Bowyer, _Philosophical Perspectives for Education_ (Glenview, Illinois: Scott Foresman and Company, 1970), p. 123; and W. T. Jones, _A History of Western Philosophy_ (New York: Harcourt Brace, 1952), pp. 194-201.

[9]Jones, _A History of Western Philosophy_, pp. 679-84.

[10]J. P. Guilford, _The Nature of Human Intelligence_ (New York: McGraw-Hill Book Company, Inc., 1967).

[11]Albert W. Upton, Design for Thinking (Palo Alto, California: Pacific Books, 1961).

[12]B. S. Bloom, D. R. Krathwohl, and B. B. Masia, Taxonomy of Educational Objectives, Handbook I: Cognitive Domain (New York: David McKay Company, Inc., 1956).

[13]More detailed treatment of the work of Upton, Bloom, and Guilford will be found in Chapters Two, Three, and Four.

[14]D. R. Krathwohl, B. S. Bloom, and B. B. Masia, Taxonomy of Educational Objectives, Handbook II: Affective Domain (New York: David McKay, Inc., 1964).

[15]Ibid.; Bloom, et al., Cognitive Domain; and A. J. Harrow, A Taxonomy of the Psychomotor Domain (New York: David McKay Company, Inc., 1972).

CHAPTER II--<u>Intellectual</u> <u>Endeavors</u>:
The <u>King</u> <u>of</u> <u>the</u> <u>Domains</u>

HISTORICAL DEVELOPMENT OF THE COGNITIVE DOMAIN

At some lost moment in history, the first primitive being thought about thinking. Instead of focusing upon a task at hand, his thought pattern dwelt upon the process of cognition itself. Since that first beginning, man has made consistent attempts to make sense out of making sense.

Psychologists often point to René Descartes (1596-1650) as an early pioneer in identifying the function of the mind. Descartes broke down human behavior into two categories; "voluntary" and "involuntary." Involuntary behavior was a response to the immediate environment, such as removing a hand from a hot pan. But the voluntary category offered more interest, because Descartes said that humans were able to influence body actions through use of the mind. The brain, therefore, could initiate action, and behavior could be sorted by whether the behavior was or was not initiated by the mind.

The "involuntary" category, however, was the area most pursued during the next two hundred years. Often, investigators became intrigued with reflex action, and work centered upon animal intelligence.

Of particular interest are efforts such as those of Thorndike in developing "The Law of Effect." It is referred to here because of its relationship to the first level of the classification scheme outlined later in this chapter. "The early work of Thorndike (1898) on escape from puzzle boxes grew out of the search for evidence of mental processes in animals, but led to the statement of a fundamental principle of so-called goal-directed behavior that did not imply any form of mental action. In a standard experiment, Thorndike studied the process by which a cat learned to escape from a box by operating a latch. Initially, the cat scrambled about until it hit the release mechanism, which allowed it to run out of the box and obtain food. During subsequent trials, the cat's latency to operate the latch became shorter and shorter, and its movements became smoother and more efficient. The process could be described by saying that the cat initially tried out various responses until one succeeded, and then used its experience in order to gain access to food as soon as possible on each trial. Thorndike viewed matters differently, however. In his view, the consequences of the cat's movements-- freedom and food--had served to stamp in a connection between the stimuli of the box and the particular movements that in the past had been followed immediately by release. The stamping in of connections was entirely automatic and independent of any comprehension of the release mechanism and its operation by the latch. Thus, the emphasis was shifted from the purpose of the cat's actions to the past consequence of similar actions." Thorndike termed the underlying principle The Law of Effect.[1]

"The Law of Effect is that: of several responses made to the same situation, those which are accompanied or closely followed by satisfaction to the animal will, other things being equal, be more firmly connected with the situation, so that, when it recurs, they will be less likely to occur."[2]

From these early investigations into the function of the mind, psychology developed various learning theories, concepts of intelligence, and classifications of mental operations. E. R. Guthrie (1886-1960), E. C. Tolman (1886-1961), C. L. Hull (1884-1952), and B. F. Skinner (1904-) all developed theories of behavior which attempted to explain how the mind responds to stimuli and directs behavior.

Psychologists intrigued with measuring intelligence also contributed to an understanding of mental processes. The beginnings of testing of intelligence are usually traced to the late nineteenth and early twentieth centuries and Alfred Binet's work for the French government to devise a procedure for the detection of retardation in young children. In 1905, 1908, and 1911, Binet and T. Simon published scales of performance tests. By 1916 this effort had been adapted after revisions by Lewis Termin at Stanford University. This initial Stanford-Binet was followed by many group and individual intelligence measurement devices.

This is mentioned because in order to measure intelligence scholars first had to hypothesize what it was, thus leading to classification schemes for mental operations. For instance, Spearman's[3] theory that there is a general, or "g" factor that influences all intelligence and that there are many special or "s" factors, preceded the theory of Thurstone that there are a number of primary factors such as ability to deal with spatial relations, number ability, word fluency, and vocabulary.[4] Such theories have helped lead to various attempts to classify cognitive abilities and acts.

POSSIBLE CLASSIFICATION SCHEMES
FOR OBJECTIVES

UPTON'S "DESIGN FOR THINKING"

Albert Upton, now retired, but formerly Chairman of the English Department and Director of General Studies at Whittier College in California, attracted considerable attention within the academic community a few years ago through replicated studies which showed that systematic study of his materials consistently increased the intelligence scores of college freshmen an average of 10 IQ points.[5]

Upton's primary intention was to have students think more clearly by increasing their understanding of how language works. In the process, he developed a tri-category system of classifying all human endeavors into categories labeled as "sensory," "affective," and "logical."

The sensory category has to do with all "sensory" input into the brain. The affective category accommodates emotions, and the logical category handles the cognitive skills.

15

Within the logical category, Upton describes four basic operations. The first of these is "qualification," wherein objects and data are identified and stored in the memory bank. When the data are manipulated in any cognitive way, they then are being analyzed in one of three ways: classification, structural analysis, and operational analysis.

Classification is the act of grouping things into types, and answers the questions: "What is this a sort of, and what are the sorts of this?"

Structural analysis is the act of seeing sections of objects, and answers the questions: "What is this a part of, and what are the parts of this?"

Operational analysis is the act of organizing events in time and space, and answers the questions: "What is this a stage of, and what are the stages of this?"

Although not intended at its inception for such a purpose, this category system could be used as a classification scheme to ensure that objectives identified by teachers as being worthy of teaching range through a variety of intellectual skill areas.

GUILFORD'S "STRUCTURE OF INTELLECT"

Guilford's Structure of Intellect (SOI) model is the result of many years of research concerned with identifying human intellectual traits and determining the ways in which the traits (or abilities) occur in relation to one another. The model is a three-way classification of 120 intellectual abilities. The three dimensions are contents, operations, and products. The classification scheme helps to clarify the intellectual processes that take place when an individual learns; that is, how an individual's mind discriminates, processes, and stores information.[6]

The contents dimension of the model classifies the types of information that an individual is capable of discriminating and processing (i.e., figural, symbolic, semantic, and behavioral information). The operations dimension classifies the ways in which an individual processes the information he has discriminated (i.e., cognition, memory, divergent production, convergent production, and evaluation). The <u>products</u> dimension classifies the organization or form the information takes after it has been discriminated and processed. The SOI model is presented in the form of a cube in Figure 1.

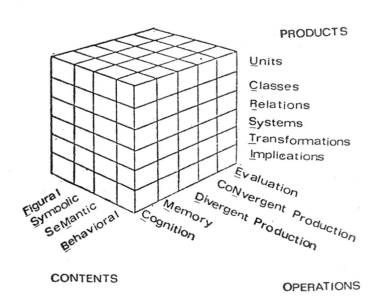

Guilford's Structure of Intellect[7]
Figure 1

Each of the 120 intellectual abilities is a combination of the three dimensions. (For example, combining an operation, a type of content, and a product to form the ability, <u>Cognition of Figural Units</u>, or <u>Evaluation of Behavioral Implications</u>.) A number of combinations are identified within the evaluation operations matrix in Figure 2.

	Units	Classes	Relations	Systems	Transformation	Implications
FIGURAL	Evaluation of Figural Units				Evaluation of Figural Transformations	
SYMBOLIC			Evaluation of Symbolic Relations		Evaluation of Symbolic Transformations	
SEMANTIC					Evaluation of Semantic Transformations	
BEHAVIORAL	Evaluation of Behavioral Units	Evaluation of Behavioral Classes	Evaluation of Behavioral Relations	Evaluation of Behavioral Systems	Evaluation of Behavioral Transformations	Evaluation of Behavioral Implications

Samples of Cell Titles in the Evaluation Operations
Matrix (Structure of Intellect)

Figure 2

GAGNÉ'S ANALYSIS OF INSTRUCTIONAL OBJECTIVES

In order to assist in the design of learning activities, Robert Gagné defined a series of categories that

18

can be helpful to teachers in order to classify human
behaviors. Gagné pointed to a first basic form of
learning called "response differentiation." This level
of behavior is the single act of repeating after a cue
a mimicking response. Examples of learning based on
responses can be found in the foreign language and
music classes of any secondary school.[8]

Second, "associations" are those activities in
which there is a different response than the cue. For
instance, in a Spanish class a teacher's greeting
"Buenos días" followed by a mimicking "Buenos días" by
the student is a "response." When followed by a student "Good morning," it is an "association."

The third form, "identification," requires that
the responding individual make a "variety of different
responses to an equal number of stimuli." This classification is essentially a one-to-one relationship between two sets: a set of stimuli and a set of responses. When assembling a radio from a schematic
drawing, each part has a part number that corresponds
to the drawing.

A fourth learning form, "sequences," often exists
within sets of behaviors. Some of these behavior
chains are quite common. The sequences exhibited by
good drivers are consistent enough so that many driver
education courses now use behavior chains to educate
teachers to train students. This sequence of correct
behavior needed to drive well is labeled by the instructor as chains. A chain, after seating, might be
to adjust the seat for comfort, fasten seat belt, adjust mirror, and so on.

Fifth, "classification" of objects is identified
by Gagné. This is the generally understood meaning of
the term, and denotes the ability of the student, when
presented objects or ideas, to categorize them with
other objects or ideas with similar characteristics.

"Principles" or "rules" acquisition as a common
learning task in the school is the sixth type identified. It implies that the student can apply a learned
principle. An example of an applied principle would
not only be the ability to repeat "I before E except
after C," but to apply this rule in spelling correctly
and to know when not to use it through memorization of
the exceptions. In notation, a principle can be
described as the chaining of two concepts: if a, then
b.

Finally, "strategies" are forms of behavior in which principles are chained together. When the quarterback of the football team looks at the defensive line-ups of the opposition, he has a series of principles running through his head, i.e., "If the defensive halfback is too close to the line we should run swing pass 'x' and if the line is over-shifted to the right, we should run counterplay 'y'."

But when both conditions occur, the quarterback must begin to "chain" his principles in the order in which he thinks he can score the easiest. Such chaining becomes a strategy.

BLOOM'S TAXONOMY OF EDUCATIONAL OBJECTIVES

The final categorical scheme reviewed here is the well-known and used Taxonomy of Educational Objectives: Cognitive Domain.[9]

Bloom has broken down the "cognitive domain" into six levels. Unlike Upton and Guilford, but similar to Gagné, these categories are arranged in an hierarchical order. The lowest level is called "Knowledge." At this level the student simply memorizes and recalls. The second level is called "Comprehension." Here the student can understand the material and perhaps can explain it or summarize it.

"Application" follows. It is the use of a set of rules, principles, or methods to accomplish a task. The fourth level has been labeled "Analysis." Analysis means to break down things into parts by identifying the similarities and differences between the parts.

"Synthesis" is the putting together of ideas or objects so as to construct a new whole. And finally, "Evaluation" is to make judgments about the worth of given material or a method for a specific purpose.

SUMMARY

Several methods have been presented, each of which could be used to classify objectives. Some of these, however, were not developed specifically for this purpose, and those that were have not been linked to a comparative classification in the psychomotor and affective domains. The following classification allows for this contingency.

THE PIERCE-GRAY CLASSIFICATION MODEL
FOR THE COGNITIVE DOMAIN

In presenting the following scheme, the authors are operating with several assumptions. First, any classification must be based upon the work of others, and this one is no exception. Second, the classification must be useable for teachers. That is, it must have sufficient levels to allow the teacher to use it to ensure a variety of intellectual tasks, but not be so complex that it is burdensome to learn to use. Third, it must be arranged so that the basic classification is analogous and transferable to the psycho-motor and affective domains.

Throughout this book the word "level" is used to identify a succeeding category. This is a convenience, and only implies a hierarchy within a specified content area. For instance, the ability to understand, describe, and explain the theory of relativity involves more cognition than the ability to judge which dress is more appropriate for a social occasion. The second objective is classified at a lower "level" in the classification scheme than the first. However, the application of the theory of relativity, or synthesizing a new theory, would take more cognition than the explanation of the theory. Thus, content can be of assistance in determining the amount of cognitive effort.

The authors also consider the ability to identify similarities and differences between things as the basic intellectual skill upon which all thought is based.[10] What is being cognated, and for what purpose, determines the categories. In this regard, all classification schemes are artificial and arbitrary. They are tools to be used. The following tool is presented as one that can be used easily by teachers to good advantage as an aid in planning, teaching, and assessment.

LEVEL I: COGNITIVE PERCEIVING

What is it that makes up the fundamental cognitive ingredient? Perhaps one of the most penetrating analyses of this question was made over a century ago by Charles Kay Ogden and I. A. Richards in their essay The Meaning of Meaning,[1] and became a basic component of Upton's Design for Thinking. Meaning, or perception, is the process of identifying an entity. But "nothing ever means itself alone; it can only be meaningful to somebody about something else. Meaning, then, is simply a function of the cortex in action; it is what goes on in a brain when it makes a connection between two or more things. . . . A unit of meaning-- that is, a meaning that cannot at the moment be practically broken up into two or more lesser meanings--is made up of a thing and the relation which connects it to another thing. . . . [I]n order to be conscious of a finite thing . . . , we must have at least two other things: a boundary and another infinite or indefinite thing. . . ."[12]

"This means that the first moment of consciousness [Perception] takes place when the meaningful moment is connected with previously experienced but meaningless moments by the image symbol. It is therefore by no means nonsensical to say that when we are conscious of any given experience for the first time, we must be conscious of at least one other experience similar to it, likewise for the first time. [Perception is] simply that first act of signaling the resemblance of the two now-meaningful experiences to one another by what we have called a genus term."[13]

It now becomes clear why the quotation from Nevin, et al., regarding Thorndike's "Law of Effect" was referred to at the beginning of this chapter. Attempts to deal with animal intelligence seem to define such intelligence as being very close to our definition of Perception, but without the crucial factor of language. Language allows us the ability to apply the genus term to similar experiences. Hence, an essential difference between man and the animals is identified.

The organism is born with sensing organs and systems that might be thought of as the "machinery for keeping in touch" with the environment. This "machinery" transmits impulses which enable the brain to attach meaning to experience and thereby gradually develop a potential (or readiness) for acting. Each new Perception or moment of meaning increases this action potential. This potential can be viewed from three different, but related, frames of reference; namely, (1) potential for data manipulation (the Cognitive

Action Potential), (2) potential for "feeling" or emoting (the Affective Action Potential), and (3) potential for muscular movement and motion (the Psychomotor Action Potential). In the Pierce-Gray classification model, Level I, of all three learning domains, is concerned with the development (or creation) of the organism's action potential--and Level II is the "activating" category for all domains.

Before proceeding further, it seems imperative to make a distinction between the hereditary set (and involuntary reflexes) of the developing organism, and the beginnings of learning. The newborn infant inherits certain reflexes and response patterns that come into play automatically as it is bombarded by environmental stimuli. Thus, at birth, the organism can be thought of as an undifferentiated blend of sensations, uncontrolled movements, and unsorted nerve cell impulses. This classification model makes no attempt to deal with this pre-conscious phase of the infant's experience, but rather, it begins at that point where the first moment of meaning occurs.

For this classification scheme, Cognitive Perceiving is defined as the student's ability to (1) identify bits and pieces of data, and (2) store them in the memory bank. Much of this is done in terms of words or other symbols, and the initial development of this ability takes place at an early age. One could draw a parallel to the work of Piaget. The initial development of Perception could be thought of as the process of assimilation and accommodation of data on the child's growing schemata. In students, this basic ability in isolating and inputing into the brain in the form of language and other symbols has begun long before they reach the classroom. Objectives are seldom written at this level by regular classroom teachers.

Sublevel 1.1--Focusing

To further define these operations, sublevel 1.1--Focusing, is described as being the moment at which meaning first comes into existence because of the perception of relations (such as "figure-ground" relationships or "thing, boundary, other thing" distinctions).

Sublevel 1.2--Storing

Sublevel 1.2--Storing, then logically follows as the distinctions and item identifications (i.e., Cognitive Action Potential) are inputed into the storage system of the brain, usually through the use of language and the genus term.

LEVEL II: UNDERSTANDING

At the Understanding level, the individual retrieves input and begins to manipulate the data on cue. He comprehends a request or circumstances and can withdraw from the brain appropriate items. He can demonstrate the retrieval by stating things word for word or he may change their form and put them in his own words. He may demonstrate his Understanding by changing information from one set of symbols to another while retaining the essential meaning. Ultimately, he is able to extract meaning and significance from information and explain how it is related to other things he has learned.

Sublevel 2.1--Retrieving

At sublevel 2.1--Retrieving, the individual understands a request for information or an appropriate time to Retrieve information and does so.

Sublevel 2.2--Rendering

At sublevel 2.2--Rendering, the individual is able to repeat (or rephrase) material in a way that is consistent with the original(s) that he has inputed. He can summarize paragraphs or outline chapters and retain the meaning. He can change content from one set of word arrangements, or combinations, to another. He can duplicate given symbols or diagrams at a later time. He can recall the appropriate English word that is synonymous with another English word or a French word.

Sublevel 2.3--Conceptualizing

At sublevel 2.3--Conceptualizing, the individual can explain the meaning and significance of data

rendered. Conceptual models are fully understood along
with their relationship to other models. The individual can explain something as simple as the relationship
of parents to children, or something as complex as the
theory of relativity and its impact on the scientific
community. This, of course, does not imply that the
content itself was necessarily inputed through any
process higher than cognitive perceiving, retrieving,
and rendering. However, it is quite likely that before a high level of Conceptualizing is reached, certain higher order skills will have come into play to
assist in the attainment of full Conceptualization.

LEVEL III: APPLYING

At the Applying level the individual uses simple
or complex rules, procedures, or principles to accomplish particular tasks.

Sublevel 3.1--Routine Application

Often an individual who is engaged in a cognitive
task can utilize simple rules, procedures, or principles in an automatic way. He is able to call the
rules up and use them with little thought. If necessary, however, explanations could be given (Rendering);
or the individual could even specify the relationship
of the principle to other principles or provide reasons for the use of the rule or principle (Conceptualizing). In actual practice, however, the rules and
principles are applied in routine fashion, without need
for concentration. Examples of such Routine Application are basic arithmetic computations, the filling out
of simple application forms (with specific directions),
playing simple games using a few rules, and use of a
routine procedure for locating specific library materials.

Sublevel 3.2--Procedural Application

The next sublevel is somewhat more complex. Here
a procedure is understood and used consistently in
varying circumstances. At this sublevel, the individual may be presented with a mathematical problem involving several computations and must remember several
rules and then use them in order to be able to derive

the correct answer. He may be able to correctly fill out a scorebook for a basketball game. Or he may translate paragraphs from Spanish to French, where words are retrieved and then a particular word arrangement (sentence structure) is developed through Procedural Application. Also, he can fill out more involved forms (e.g., federal income tax form), in which the directions (rules) are sometimes easy and sometimes more difficult; he can engage in simulations and games with involved rules; and he can use a wide variety of research procedures to gather proper input for later analysis.

Sublevel 3.3--Complex Application

At sublevel 3.3--Complex Application, the rules and procedures are so involved that some specialized training may be needed in order to properly apply them. While the layman may be able to fill out most income tax forms by the rules, there is a point at which the tax regulations are so complex that their application is almost reserved to certified public accountants. Similarly, the expertise of a chemist, mathematician, or lawyer is needed in the application of complex rules, principles, and regulations peculiar to their fields.

If, in the application of the principles, the individual must compare the uniqueness of a situation to other similar situations and deduce the more applicable rule among many possibilities, he has moved to the first sublevel of Analysis, 4.1--Comparative Analysis.

LEVEL IV: ANALYZING

Analysis can be thought of as problem solving through the identification of similarities and differences between a given problem and other problems or circumstances an individual has previously encountered. He attempts to find "the answer." An implication of Analysis is that there is either a best or a right answer that the individual should work toward.

Sublevel 4.1--Comparative Analysis

At sublevel 4.1--Comparative Analysis, the student identifies similarities and differences between sets of circumstances, descriptions, or phenomena. When asked to compare the Russian and American revolutions he can locate similar and different events, attitudes, and results.

Sublevel 4.2--Logical Analysis

At sublevel 4.2--Logical Analysis, the individual induces a rule, generalization, concept, or principle through identification of similar attributes found in a series of examples. He may find that in subtraction, when the subtrahend has a nine in the one's column, the digit in the answer in the one's column is always one more than the digit in the one's column in the minuend. If given a pile of rocks, he is able to induce three categories because metamorphic, sedimentary, and igneous rocks each have distinguishing characteristics.

Similarly, the individual uses logic and comparisons to determine answers, or uses principles, rules, generalizations, or concepts to make inferences that help to clarify or explain a particular phenomenon or relationship. When asked to explain why ice is floating in one beaker on a clear liquid and not floating in an adjacent beaker, he identifies analogous situations in his past that could explain the phenomenon and asks questions to deduce the reason why. When presented with a hypothetical math word problem, the student compares the situation to others he has experienced and deduces by trial and error the correct formulas and procedures.

LEVEL V: COGNITIVE JUDGING

In dealing with life situations, individuals just as often face circumstances in which there is not a "correct" or "right" answer as when there is. Varying from what tie to wear in the morning to the choice of an occupation, people make choices based on the data available. This process is continuous and cyclical. In order to make a judgment, criteria for making the decision must be determined through analysis and evaluation. Based on the criteria, the final decision is

27

made. Criteria are continuously being altered; thus
ultimate judgments continue to vary.

Sublevel 5.1--Establishing
Ideational Criteria

Individuals feel most comfortable in the process
of selection from alternatives when they have judged
a set of criteria as being workable and worthwhile for
them. They may even be reluctant to examine the criteria in order to make changes, because to do so may
alter a comfortable judgment process. However, in the
process of Cognitive Judging, people continually
formulate and examine sets of criteria that are used
in making choices between ideas.

Once the judgments about selection of criteria
have been established, the act of Ideational Judging
becomes possible. It may be a difficult process not
because of the final act of judgment, but because the
slate of criteria may necessarily take into account
conflicting factors. For instance, when faced with a
job offer, a presently employed person may balance
criteria including:

1. Distance to travel to work (further than at
    present);

2. Job security (slightly less than current job);

3. Salary (more money in new job);

4. Fringe benefits (better in new job);

5. Chances for promotion (slightly better in new
    job);

6. Philosophy of superiors (company- rather than
    employee-minded in new job);

7. Size of company (smaller than at present).

If the employee can judge the priorities of the criteria, the Ideational Judgment follows easily.

Sublevel 5.2--Ideational Judging
(Criteria-based Decision
from Alternatives)

At this sublevel, the individual renders his
decision based on his assembled criteria. He, if
necessary, can explain those rationales upon which the
judgment was made.

LEVEL VI: COGNITIVE CREATING

Sublevel 6.1--Uniting Ideas

When an individual begins efforts to logically
unite ideas to formulate new products, the processes
described at sublevels 5.1 and 5.2 repeat themselves,
but with a new concept or whole as the result.

When studying the relationships between ideas and
concepts, the individual determines similarities and
differences and ultimately makes judgments about how
the notions could fit together. This judgmental process of Uniting Ideas can produce, after assembly, a
product of some difference from the original pieces
when unassembled. Thus, the individual may put together a travel itinerary for a five-day trip to New
York or plan a day's menu that encompasses items from
each food group. The "parts" of the product are not
new, but the arrangement, sequence, or total configu-
ration is original for the individual. Different
individuals would produce different products simply because their judgments would be different. That is,
they would use different criteria as their basis for
selection of parts. It is possible for this process
to approach elements of creativity, but as long as the
actual combining of ideas, concepts, or principles is
based on logic and judgment, the individual is operating at sublevel 6.1--Uniting Ideas.

When operating at the leading edge of knowledge,
it is possible for the individual to allow himself
moments of ideational divergence. In these instances,
the individual may be attempting to tap into Jung's
"Collective Unconscious," allow disjointed synapses
in the brain to make connections, engage in a brainstorming session, tinker with metaphor or other devices to free the mind.

29

<u>Sublevel 6.2--Creative Insight</u>

On occasion, after being involved in the process described above, the phenomenon of genuine creativity may take place in an insightful flash. When this occurs, the individual reaches sublevel 6.2--Creative Insight.

CONCLUDING REMARKS

As was previously stated, the above classification is presented as a tool to assist teachers in formulating objectives and arranging learning activities designed to utilize and refine varying intellectual abilities of students. In reality, the process of seeing similarities and differences between new situations and old experiences, formulating criteria for making decisions, making those decisions, and their execution, is a circular process that goes on continuously and is intertwined. Picture a student who is answering a multiple-choice question that the teacher felt was at the understanding level, but which in reality covered material that was not understood. He will take all the clues in the stem and foils of the question and couple them with material that he does understand. Then he will see similarities and differences between this question and others like it (Analysis). Ultimately he determines reasons--or criteria--for his choice and judges one to be the best. The circular process goes on constantly and is all part of a larger scheme commonly called "Thinking."

SUMMARY OF LEVELS IN THE
COGNITIVE DOMAIN

I. COGNITIVE PERCEIVING

    1.1 Focusing

    1.2 Storing

II. UNDERSTANDING

    2.1 Retrieving

    2.2 Rendering

2.3 Conceptualizing

III. APPLYING

3.1 Routine Application

3.2 Procedural Application

3.3 Complex Application

IV. ANALYZING

4.1 Comparative Analysis

4.2 Logical Analysis

V. COGNITIVE JUDGING

5.1 Establishing Ideational Criteria

5.2 Ideational Judging (Criteria-based Decision from Alternatives)

VI. COGNITIVE CREATING

6.1 Uniting Ideas

6.2 Creative Insight

ENDNOTES

[1] John A. Nevin, ed., The Study of Behavior; Learning, Motivation, Emotion and Instinct (Glenview, Illinois: Scott, Foresman and Company, 1973), p. 9.

[2] E. L. Thorndike, Animal Intelligence (New York: The Macmillan Company, 1911).

[3] C. Spearman, The Abilities of Man (New York: The Macmillan Company, 1927).

[4] L. L. Thurstone and T. G. Thurstone, "Primary Mental Abilities Scale: Primary, Elementary, and Intermediate," Chicago, Science Research Associates, 1950.

[5]Albert W. Upton, _Design for Thinking_ (Palo Alto, California: Pacific Books, 1961).

[6]J. P. Guilford, _The Nature of Human Intelligence_ (New York: McGraw-Hill Book Company, Inc., 1967).

[7]George W. Etheridge, Robert E. Hedges, and Richard C. Youngs, _Teacher, Child and Curriculum: A Program for Individualizing Instruction_ (Normal, Illinois: Illinois State University, 1973), p. 47.

[8]Robert Gagné, "The Analysis of Instructional Objectives for the Design of Instruction," in _Teaching Machines and Programmed Instruction_, ed. Robert Glaser (Washington, D.C.: National Education Association, 1967), pp. 41-60.

[9]B. S. Bloom, D. R. Krathwohl, and B. B. Masia, _Taxonomy of Educational Objectives, Handbook I: Cognitive Domain_ (New York: David McKay Company, Inc., 1956).

[10]Jerome S. Bruner, et al., _A Study of Thinking_ (New York: John Wiley and Sons, Inc., 1956); and Upton, _Design for Thinking_.

[11]Charles K. Ogden and I. A. Richards, _The Meaning of Meaning_ (London, England: Routledge and Kegan Paul, Ltd., 1949), pp. 68-74.

[12]Upton, _Design for Thinking_, pp. 30-31.

[13]Ibid., p. 108. "Genus Term" as used here can be thought of as the language symbol for a concept.

CHAPTER III--<u>Affective</u> <u>Endeavors</u>:
<u>The</u> <u>Queen</u> <u>of</u> <u>the</u> <u>Domains</u>

THE AFFECTIVE DOMAIN IN
HISTORICAL PERSPECTIVE

The affective domain is most commonly associated with feelings and emotions, and is usually displayed in the form of positive or negative reactions to given events, objects, behaviors, policies, or situations. Thus, affective behaviors are those behaviors which have emotional overtones; that is, they are accompanied by varying degrees of feeling, and thereby reflect distinct "approach" or "avoidance" predispositions. Various terms are commonly employed to identify affective behaviors (or tendencies), and a sampling might include words such as like, dislike, attitude, value, belief, feeling, interest, appreciation, and characterization. An individual's past experience in interacting with the environment shapes the nature and scope of affective responses. Hence, some knowledge of another person's past experiences and present affective behavior would allow an observer to make tentative predictions about future affective behavior with varying degrees of assurance.

Over the years, teachers, scholars, philosophers, politicians, and laymen of various persuasions have been concerned with the affective domain in education. In fact, the history of education is replete with proposals and programs of wide variety designed to guide, develop, or mold the social and personal dispositions and commitments of the young. The modern concept of public education itself was conceived as a means of securing mass loyalty to the nation state. National consciousness was thought essential to the survival of

the nation, and the public schools were considered to
be proper institutions for instilling in the young
appropriate attitudes of respect and loyalty. Hence,
serious interest in the affective domain is by no means
a recent development in the field of education.

Historically, the basic approach to affective education has been two-fold. First, those ideals, attitudes, values, or behaviors were identified that were
considered essential to perpetuating the existing
social order. Second, an attempt was made to instill
in the young the appropriate affective dispositions
and behaviors by means of exhortation and/or example.
Four teaching strategies characteristic of this type
of affective education are listed below.

1. Precepts--e.g., use of precepts such as "a
   penny saved is a penny earned" as a means of
   promoting thrift;

2. Exemplars--e.g., use of stories about Abraham
   Lincoln's early life as a means of promoting
   honesty;

3. Ritual--e.g., use of the pledge of allegiance
   ritual as a means of promoting patriotism;

4. Environmentalism--e.g., use of a democratically organized classroom as a means of promoting
   the transfer of democratic behaviors to adult
   life.[1]

In using such approaches, the objectives of affective
education depend completely upon societal preference.
What the ongoing society or the school defines as the
good life becomes the version of life that young
people are taught to model. In a society that is ex-
periencing change, uncertainty, and value-conflict,
such an approach creates many problems. It leaves
young people with conflicting values (few of which
have been examined reflectively), and it fails to
supply them with a mode of analysis or method by which
conflicts might be resolved. Contemporary interest in
the affective domain is becoming increasingly
oriented toward teaching young people ways of examining and resolving the value-conflicts that presently
plague society.

AFFECTIVE DEVELOPMENT AND CONFLICT

In the process of interacting with the physical
and social environment, the human organism develops a
unique personality or self concept. The developmental
process is influenced by a tendency of the organism to
grow in the direction of what generally might be
termed psychological health and maturity. In short,
it rejects pain and embraces pleasure. Usually life
is more pleasurable if growth is made in the direction
of developing individual autonomy, actualizing individual potential, and achieving unity of personality.
Thus, the organism usually finds satisfaction and
lessens pain if it strives:

1. To become autonomous, to make its own decisions and choices in the structuring of experience;

2. To become what it is capable of becoming, to
   actualize its possibilities and potentialities; and

3. To achieve unity of personality, to blend or
   integrate experience into a coherent, unified, and consistent system of feelings,
   ideas, and attitudes.[2]

An individual who is afforded opportunities to
develop in accordance with such tendencies seemingly
will operate better if able to assimilate new experience into familiar categories of a basic structure,
and accommodate a degree of restructuring of experience
from time to time. In short, the individual builds
confidence in the ability to meet and deal with present
and future conflicts because of past success with
operational modes that have proved workable.

An individual growing up in a static or slowly
changing society gradually assimilates the cultural
traditions and learns what to expect and how to fit
into the scheme of things. The adult encounters few
experiences that cannot be easily assimilated.
Throughout a lifetime most of the experiences conform
to, or are consistent with, the model internalized as
a child or young adult. Thus, one is afforded a relatively stable climate in which to develop and maintain
a personality structure that is balanced, internally

consistent, and socially relevant.

An individual growing up in a dynamic, pluralistic, urban-industrial society encounters a vastly different set of circumstances--from both the quantitative and qualitative points of view. The young person is confronted by a variety of experiences, many of which were not a part of the pre-adult experience of elders. As adults attempt to reconcile their own past and present experiences, they may become confused as they encounter inconsistencies and contradictions. Such confusion is easily communicated to the younger generation. The result is often tension, frustration, and uncertainty for both young people and adults as well as conflict and a lessening of meaningful communication between generations. Needless to say, such a climate is not conducive to healthy psychological development; rationalization, alienation, and continued social and personal disorganization are the predictable consequences of such a conflict-ridden state of affairs.[3]

For some time there has been persuasive evidence available that a cultural crisis (which can be defined as an affective or value-crisis) is either imminent or in progress in much of the Western world.[4] Also, a good deal of knowledge has been accumulating relative to the processes involved in human valuation and cultural socialization. A number of intellectual strategies have been proposed for dealing with conflicting valuations and social controversy. Although by no means definitive, such input has brought a critical social problem into focus, has made explicit the inadequacy of current educational programs in dealing with it, and has provided a degree of insight into the possibility of a significant role for affective education in helping to resolve the problem.

ALTERNATIVE CLASSIFICATION SCHEMES

In order to plan for effective instruction in the affective domain, and to relate the three domains, it is most helpful to have available some type of model or classification system that specifies categories and/or levels of affective behavior. A number of attempts have been made to conceptualize all (or part) of the affective domain. Several of these conceptual models (or classification schemes) are presented and briefly discussed in the following paragraphs.

GUILFORD:
STRUCTURE OF INTELLECT

The Structure of Intellect model (described in more detail in Chapter Two) is most useful in describing the interrelationships between types of mental operations, types of content encountered, and various ways of organizing what has been encountered and processed. Although the SOI is basically a cognitive model, affective input is likely to be present when one engages in particular mental operations in processing certain kinds of content. In particular, the operations of <u>evaluation</u> and <u>divergent production</u> seem to have a special relationship to the affective domain. The relationship between evaluation and the various types of content and products is illustrated in Figure 2, Chapter Two. When an individual deals with behavioral content and when involved in producing transformations and implications, it may be that affective considerations influence thinking. In fact, it has been hypothesized that the affective domain might be conceptualized as a fourth dimension of the SOI model, a dimension that is both a part of each of the 120 abilities, and at the same time a connecting or unifying link between all of the abilities and dimensions of the model.[5]

RATHS: PROCESS OF VALUING

Raths and his associates developed a model which both defines the concept of value and describes the process through which individuals move in developing their values.[6] The model also includes a set of sub-value behaviors (or value indicators). In general, Raths views value development as an integral part of intelligent self-directed behavior; the striving of the individual to actualize full human potential. The three components of the model are summarized below.

<u>Definition of Values</u>--Those beliefs, purposes, attitudes, and so on, that are chosen freely and thoughtfully, prized, and acted upon.

<u>Process of Valuing</u>--The process used by the individual in developing values includes choosing, prizing,

and acting in the following schema:

Choosing: 1. Freely;

2. From alternatives;

3. After thoughtful consideration of the consequences of each alternative;

Prizing: 4. Cherishing, being happy with the choice;

5. Willing to affirm the choice publicly;

Acting: 6. Doing something with the choice;

7. Repeatedly, in some pattern of life.

Unless the above process has been operative with respect to a given belief, purpose, or attitude, it has not become a value for the individual (or unless something satisfied all seven "criteria" above it is not defined as a value).

Value Indicators--Categories of behavior that might be termed subvalues. They might in some instances indicate the presence of a value, but usually they indicate something less than a value (i.e., something that has not been brought up to the level of the valuing process). The eight value indicator categories are as follows:

1. Goals or purposes;

2. Aspirations;

3. Attitudes;

4. Interests;

5. Feelings;

6. Beliefs and convictions;

7. Activities;

8. Worries, problems, obstacles.

The Raths model is primarily a description of the means through which individuals internalize their values. True values are the product of experience and rational thought. Such values should be effective in relating the individual to his world in a satisfying and intelligent manner.

MASLOW: HIERARCHY
OF THE NEEDS OF MAN

Maslow viewed human personality as a dynamic entity seeking to actualize its potentialities within the context of a given physical and social environment. He further maintained that a sound theoretical and empirical case can be made in support of the idea that individuals are naturally motivated in the direction of self-actualization. For him, healthy personality growth and development was synonymous with the progressive satisfaction of certain basic needs. According to Maslow, "these needs or values are related to each other in a hierarchial and developmental way, in an order of strength and of priority . . . all these basic needs may be considered to be simply steps along the . . . path to general self-actualization . . . it looks as if there were a single ultimate value for mankind, a far goal toward which all men strive."[7]

According to Maslow's theory of human needs, man's basic needs can be arranged in a hierarchy which applies to most people in most situations. There are, however, individual differences. Generally, when the first need is met by a person, he moves on to the next one, and so forth. Arranged in order of primary importance, these basic human needs are as summarized below.[8]

1. Physiological Needs--The human body needs certain things or conditions in order to survive in a hostile environment. The basic essentials that are usually included here are food, clothing, and shelter. A more comprehensive list would include the following:

   a. Food and liquid (satisfying hunger and thirst;

   b. Temperature regulation (satisfied by shelter and clothing;

c. Evacuation of waste matter;

d. Reproduction of species.

2. <u>Safety Needs</u>--Human beings need confidence in
    their ability to continue to survive in a com-
    plex (and often hostile) world; and they need
    the feeling of security which results from
    such confidence. In essence, they seek to
    alleviate uncertainty and increase certainty
    about life in general. They ring themselves
    with a variety of ceremonies, rules, and for-
    mulas which have the effect of helping them
    to be less fearful in a hostile world. Many
    of these ceremonies, rules, and formulas are
    the basis for man's religion and/or philosophy
    of life.

<u>Men seek to avoid</u>:   <u>Men seek to find</u>:

a. Pain;   a. Ways of reducing
                             risks and dangers;
b. Discomfort;
                         b. Regularities so that
c. Threatening   they will know better
    circumstances;   what to expect;

d. Uncertainty.   c. Explanations for that
                             which seems mysteri-
                             ous;

                         d. Their place in the
                             scheme of things.

3. <u>Belongingness and Love</u> Needs--Human beings
    need the confidence and the feeling of secu-
    rity which results from satisfying personal
    and social relationships. They need affec-
    tion from others and the feeling of security
    that results from such affection. They need
    to give as well as receive such affection.
    These needs consist in large part of that
    hard-to-define reciprocal condition called
    "love" (i.e., the kind of thing personified
    by such individuals as Gandhi, Christ, Buddha,
    Lincoln, Florence Nightingale, and Albert
    Schweitzer). The needs include such things
    as love or affection for (<u>or from</u>) family,
    community, or nation, desire for children,
    desire for acceptance, friendship,

companionship, and so forth.

4. <u>Esteem</u> <u>Needs</u>--Human beings need the respect of both themselves and others; this leads to self-confidence and a feeling of deserved respect. Such terms as esteem, achievement, status, fame, prestige, and recognition are descriptive of this category. Essentially, this is the need for self-respect and the respect of others.

5. <u>Self-actualization</u> <u>Needs</u>--This is the need for a human being to be what he can be, or live up to his potential, in order to be at peace with himself. Such things as self-expression, self-fulfillment, and a sense of growing or becoming something are descriptive of this category.

The following two needs are considered somewhat tentative. Their <u>strength</u> and <u>placement</u> in the hierarchy are less certain, according to Maslow.

6. <u>Knowledge</u> <u>and</u> <u>Understanding</u> <u>Needs</u>--This is the need for a human being to learn about and understand himself and the things around him; his need to seek truth! It is much more than mere academic learning. It might well be termed, <u>curiosity</u>!

7. <u>Aesthetic</u> <u>Needs</u>--This is perhaps the weakest of the seven needs, and may not appear at all in some human beings. It is the need to be surrounded by things which the individual feels are beautiful (i.e., things which excite admiring pleasure in him).

Thus, Maslow's hierarchy provides a psychological model for viewing affective development. Of particular interest to the teacher is the distinction it makes between higher- and lower-level needs, and the effect of unmet needs at a lower level on the fulfillment of needs at a higher level.

BROUDY: INTRINSIC AND
INSTRUMENTAL VALUING

The underlying striving for unity (or motive force) of the organism is termed the <u>appetitive</u> <u>principle</u> by

Broudy. The hallmarks or dimensions of the good life are the principles of self-determination, self-realization, and self-integration. The appetitive principle refers to the unsettled state of the organism brought about by desire, want, and need. The quality of life is determined by the form that the appetitive principle takes. For Broudy, self-determination is to choose on rational grounds; self-realization is to choose rationally among our potentialities; and self-integration is to remove rationally so far as possible the conflicts among our choices.[9]

Broudy proposes a way of looking at the value choices facing the individual that brings into sharp focus the conflicts between desire, want, and need. He maintains that our values indicate what we yearn for, what we succumb to, what we are willing to endure, and what we hate.

We yearn for: Things that are intrinsically positive (good in themselves); Things that are instrumentally positive (lead to a good);

We succumb to: Things that are intrinsincally positive (good in themselves); Things that are instrumentally negative (lead to a bad);

We endure: Things that are intrinsically negative (bad in themselves; Things that are instrumentally positive (lead to a good);

We hate: Things that are intrinsically negative (bad in themselves); Things that are instrumentally negative (lead to a bad).[10]

KRATHWOHL: AFFECTIVE DOMAIN TAXONOMY

Krathwohl and his associates have developed a taxonomy of affective objectives which has become quite popular with educators. It is hierarchical in form and generally utilizes the concept of internalization as the basic sorting factor between categories. The taxonomy is summarized below with a description of categories in the affective domain.[11]

1. Receiving--"At this level we are concerned
    that the learner be sensitized to the exis-
    tence of certain phenomena and stimuli; that
    is, that he be willing to receive or to at-
    tend to them." The category is divided into
    three subcategories as follows:

    1.1 Awareness;

    1.2 Willingness to Receive;

    1.3 Controlled or Selected Attention.

2. Responding--"At this level we are concerned
    with responses which go beyond merely attend-
    ing to the phenomenon. The student is suffi-
    ciently motivated that he is not just
    1.2 Willing to Attend, but perhaps it is
    correct to say that he is actively attend-
    ing. . . . The student is committing himself
    in some small measure to the phenomena in-
    volved." The category is divided into three
    subcategories as follows:

    2.1 Acquiescence in Responding;

    2.2 Willingness to Respond;

    2.3 Satisfaction in Response.

3. Valuing--"Behavior categorized at this level
    is sufficiently consistent and stable to have
    taken on the characteristics of a belief or an
    attitude. The learner displays this behavior
    with sufficient consistency in appropriate
    situations that he comes to be perceived as
    holding a value." The category is divided in-
    to three subcategories as follows:

    3.1 Acceptance of a Value;

    3.2 Preference for a Value;

    3.3 Commitment.

4. Organization--"This category is intended as
    the proper classification for objectives which
    describe the beginnings of the building of a
    value system. It is subdivided into two
    levels, since a prerequisite to interrelating

is the conceptualization of the value in a form which permits organization." The two subcategories are as follows:

4.1 Conceptualization of a Value;

4.2 Organization of a Value System.

5. Characterization By a Value or Value Complex--"At this level of internalization the values already have a place in the individual's value hierarchy, are organized into some kind of internally consistent system, have controlled the behavior of the individual for a sufficient time that he has adapted to behaving this way." The category is divided into two subcategories as follows:

5.1 Generalized Set;

5.2 Characterization.

CONCLUSIONS ABOUT APPROACHES TO THE AFFECTIVE DOMAIN

The foregoing summaries illustrate that a variety of approaches have been taken in viewing the affective domain. In the case of Guilford, the Structure of Intellect was designed almost exclusively to deal with the intellectual processes. Subsequently, educators and psychologists began to analyze the model in terms of its relationship to the affective domain, and hypothesized the links alluded to earlier. This might be called the "Cognition followed by Affect" phenomenon.

The Raths approach is essentially an example of an operational definition of the process through which individuals struggle as they cope with the problem of making choices between competing values. In a sense, it is akin to the Krathwohl work, which deals mainly with the process of value development, even though it is termed a taxonomy of the affective domain.

Maslow's theory, on the other hand, is a psychological approach that is often used in psychological circles to explain the types of intrinsic motivation (affects) that serve as the driving force behind most human behavior. Broudy's ideas might be thought of as an operationalization of the ways individuals think and react as they go about fulfilling their needs within the context of Maslow's schema.

The various approaches and ideas that have been presented provide useful information and insights into the dimensions of the affective domain. Although no single approach offers a comprehensive view of affective behavior, elements from several of the schemes might be incorporated into an affective domain classification model useful to the practicing teacher.

THE PIERCE-GRAY CLASSIFICATION MODEL FOR THE AFFECTIVE DOMAIN

THE NEED FOR AN EFFECTIVE AFFECTIVE CLASSIFICATION MODEL

The classification model for the affective domain that follows has been developed primarily to provide the practicing teacher with a useful conceptual tool. Within the model are elements from several classification systems, some of which have been alluded to earlier.

When one deals with the classification of objectives--or any system of classification for that matter--it is important to maintain consistent sorting factors. For instance, when classifying plants the task is made much simpler if a single sorting factor is used at a given level. Examples of plant sorting factors might be annual or perennial, color, shape of leaves, or size. If the person who sorts out the plants at times classifies by color and at times by size, the task becomes hopelessly confused.

Such has been one of the problems in dealing with objectives in the affective domain. Since <u>one</u> <u>must</u> <u>use</u> <u>behavioral</u> <u>evidence</u> <u>to</u> <u>substantiate</u> <u>affects</u> (i.e., it is not possible to look into the brain to <u>see</u> affects or affective changes, one may only <u>see</u> behavioral evidence), affective objectives have often been sorted into levels through use of the behavior (i.e., responses of students), through use of the affect (i.e., value to students), or blends between the two.

45

In other descriptions of student responses within the affective domain, attempts have been made to describe the steps (or process) through which the student moves in adopting a value or values, without regard to the many other facets of the affective component. In such instances, the classification system becomes an operational analysis of the stages and phases of the valuing process.

What has been lacking is a classification model for the affective domain that (1) uses a consistent sorting factor, (2) allows for an array of affects (i.e., feelings, emotions, as well as values) throughout the entire affective domain, and (3) allows for effective utilization by practicing teachers.

In structuring such criteria in order to develop a model, it first becomes obvious that the sorting factor used must be related primarily to the affect rather than the behavior. As evidence of interest in a subject matter area, the student may engage in such a wide variety of approach and avoidance behaviors that it becomes virtually impossible to describe them all. The teacher must identify the affective component needing attention, and then utilize any of many possible behaviors as evidence of an affect or affective change.

Once a decision is made to use affects themselves as the focus for classifying affective objectives, it is possible to employ any of several sorting factors. For instance, the degree of intensity could be used. In this scheme, a rage would be more intense than a reaction. Hatred would be more intense than interest. Another possible sorting factor might be duration. In this classification, a feeling that education is important would last longer than wanting to see a film. Wishing to assist a candidate for office would last longer than being irritated at traffic patterns.

However, after an examination of several factors, most can be rejected using the third criterion. That is, they may well be consistent and useable for classifying the entire domain, but they are not useful to teachers in a practical sense.

A sorting factor that does fulfill all three criteria is the degree of cognition that is used by the student when dealing with the affect. In this scheme, the behavior is used only as the means to determine

46

that degree. This may initially appear contradictory
to the reader because of the commonly encountered contention that the cognitive, affective, and psychomotor
domains are discrete entities. However, today most
educators agree that such distinctions are artificial
and hold that the domains are by no means mutually ex-
clusive. It is herein assumed that in most of the
behaviors in which people engage, the affective domain
influences cognitive decisions, and affective responses
are influenced by the intellect.

The varying amounts of cognition that the individual can use when dealing with a situation that has
affective overtones can be represented on a continuum.
This is depicted by Figure 3.

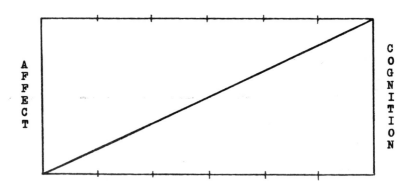

Placement of Issue or Situation
Figure 3

RELATIONSHIP OF AFFECTIVE
AND COGNITIVE DOMAINS

For a particular situation, it may be possible
for an individual to be totally cognitive in his approach. If this were the case, he would be operating
at the extreme right end of the continuum. In another
set of circumstances, an individual may be completely
emotionally dominated, and be unable to deal with the
situation intellectually at all. This would place

47

that instance at the extreme left of the continuum.
For the most part, in a given situation, people operate somewhere between the two extremes.

In spite of the continuum of blend between the
two domains, for purposes of classifying affects, it
is convenient to give various affective levels different labels. This assists one in conceptualizing segments of the affective domain, but presents the problem of assuming that every affect must fall into a
labeled segment, when in fact a given affect may border
at the edge of two levels. The benefit exceeds the
danger, however, and therefore levels and labels have
been used in this model.

Recent developments in the study of the brain
have tentatively identified different functions for
the left and right hemispheres of the brain (i.e.,
cerebrum). It has been hypothesized that the left
hemisphere is oriented toward cognition, whereas the
right hemisphere has an affective orientation. This
distinction emerges as a useful device for conceptualizing the brain's functions (see Chapter Eight). Although this notion has not been fully substantiated,
it will be used occasionally in this and later chapters for purposes of illustration and convenience.

LEVEL I: AFFECTIVE PERCEIVING

As with the lowest level in the cognitive domain,
it must be remembered that the sensory apparatus has
conveyed signals to the brain for input. These sensory
signals may impress the left hemisphere (cognitive) or
the right hemisphere (affective). As discussed in
Chapter Two, the first moment of meaning is cognitive,
and future inputs of similar stimuli may be routinely
processed by the left hemisphere (i.e., cognitively).
However, when the first moment of meaning occurs, it
will be accompanied by a set of circumstances that
may influence the right hemisphere, thereby altering
the way in which such inputs are processed in the
future. Hence, if the original stimulus is of sufficient intensity and magnitude, then the next similar
input may initiate an emotive response automatically,
without a cognitive qualification.

Sublevel 1.1--Emotive Imprinting

The process of affective perception may be broken down into two stages. The first, sublevel 1.1--Emotive Imprinting, is described above. The sensory machinery transmits impulses to the right hemisphere, which receives the input.

Sublevel 1.2--Response Setting

The sensing process sets the stage for sublevel 1.2--Response Setting, where the brain begins to build a capacity or readiness for reaction (i.e., Affective Action Potential). This "imprinting" creates an inclination--an emerging predisposition or affective set--that may influence later emotive reactions. If there has been a predominant imprint, a fixation may occur which creates an affective action potential that may later produce involuntary emotive reactions.

As noted above, the individual operating at the Affective Perceiving level is responding internally to experience. Therefore, conventional instructional objectives would not be developed for this level. External responses at the next level (i.e., Reacting), provide an indication of the extent to which Affective Perceiving has occurred.

LEVEL II: REACTING

The basic human emotion is a generalized state of excitement which can be described as undifferentiated emotion. Gradually the infant is able to differentiate more specific emotions from this general state of emotional excitement. The earliest differentiations are the emotions of distress and delight. Distress can be defined as excited avoidance behavior, whereas delight can be categorized as excited approach (or audience) behavior. The two basic patterns of human emotional response are derived from these beginnings. The simple emotional responses of infants are merely refinements of the emotions of distress and delight. These two emotional patterns also can be discerned in the behavior of older children and adults, even though emotional responses have become rather complex and, hence, are more likely to be blends of both emotional and intellectual experiences. Some of the terms used to imply various emotions derived from the two patterns of development are as follows:

Distress	Delight
Anger (and Rage)	Elation
Disgust (and Dislike)	Affection
Fear	Joy (and Surprise)
Jealousy	Euphoria
Shame (and Embarrassment)	Nostalgia

As previously discussed, the potential for emotional response (i.e., Affective Action Potential) is developed at the Affective Perceiving level. At the Reacting level, the Affective Action Potential is expressed through emotional behavior and the individual gradually becomes aware of its existence, understands how it is activated, and is able to exercise a degree of control over it. Thus, the affective potential is activated, recognized, and brought under control at the Reacting level.

Sublevel 2.1--Emoting

As commonly used, the term "emotion" implies a low level or lack of cognition; hence, the concept seems appropriate as a label for the basic affective reaction. It would include those instances where an individual is apparently unable (albeit, temporarily) to cognate about a situation. The individual undergoing the reaction does not cognitively decide what the emotion will be--he simply engages in it!

Often the reason for the emotional reaction may be difficult or impossible for an observer to discern. However, in certain circumstances the cause-effect relationship is more easily identified than in others. For instance, an emotion such as rage implies no, or almost no cognition, and the reason for the rage may be totally obscured to the observer. However, in the case of surprise or embarrassment, the stimulus may be rather obvious.

If an emotive reaction continues to reoccur over and over again, it may be thought of as an emotional trait--i.e., one in which the affective "imprint" dominates. In such instances the individual may become increasingly aware of it, perhaps between exhibitions of the reaction. However, he still may be unaware of its cause, and has very little or no control over its existence.

Thus, emotional displays, whether singular or repetitive, which are apparently involuntary and are accompanied by little or no cognition on the part of the individual, will be classified at sublevel 2.1-- Emoting.

It is at this sublevel that the spectrum of deep-seated psychological problems enter into the affective model. An in-depth analysis of such problems is the province of the specialist in mental hygiene and beyond the scope of this book. For the practicing teacher, occasional emotional outbursts at the emoting sublevel are encountered as a matter of course in teaching. When these are not repetitive, they are of little concern as long as the behavior exhibited is not harmful. However, when repetitive outbursts are encountered, the teacher must decide if the behavior is detrimental to the class and, if so, if it can be altered through teacher attention or whether the assistance of a specialist is needed.

Sublevel 2.2--Recognizing

At this sublevel, cognition emerges as an important factor in relation to the individual's emotional reactions. Also, the reasons for the reactions become easier for an observer to identify. When the student exhibits reactions that are repetitive and involuntary, but can be made increasingly aware of their existence and cause, he is operating at sublevel 2.2--Recognizing.

The emotional reactions at this sublevel are of a nature that allow the individual to discuss them soon after their occurrence with some degree of cognition. In addition, the student's level of awareness may be of sufficient magnitude for the teacher to begin assisting him in discerning possible causes (or reasons) for the reactions.

The teacher can make use of many student reactions at this sublevel as initial learning stimuli in the classroom. The resourceful teacher can utilize many

such reactions for purposes of set induction prior to
full cognitive understanding.

Sublevel 2.3--Controlling

As awareness and understanding increase, the
individual may be prompted to begin thinking about
altering a reaction in some way, combining it with
other reactions, or even eliminating it. Such concerns imply that the individual is now ready to bring
an emotional reaction more fully under control. Hence,
he has moved to sublevel 2.3--Controlling. At this
level, the student further clarifies his emotional
reactions, gains a degree of control over their existence, and begins to think about their continued existence, alteration, or elimination with reference to his
personal comfort and satisfaction.

LEVEL III: CONFORMING

After being activated, recognized, and controlled
at the Reacting level, many emotional reactions become
well-established predispositions or attitudes that
consistently pattern behavior at the Conforming level.
Ultimately, social pressures and expectations prompt
the individual to seek out convenient ways to rationalize his attitudes and behavior.

Sublevel 3.1--Artificial Attitude

After gaining a degree of control over his emotional reactions, the individual begins to develop
preferences and attitudinal predispositions toward
particular ideas, situations, and behaviors. He can
describe what his preferences are in relation to suggested ideas and he is fully aware of the attitudinal
stance from which he operates, but he can give virtually no reasons for his position(s). When asked why he
likes something he is likely to respond by merely
articulating his preference differently or in stronger
terms. For example, when asked to discuss his attitude
about ecology, he merely states that he likes the idea
of environmental preservation, but cannot readily supply reasons for holding such an attitude. Thus, when
an individual is apparently satisfied and comfortable
with the attitudinal stance he has assumed, and is
either disinclined or unable to provide reasons for

holding it, he is operating at sublevel 3.1--Artificial Attitude.

Sublevel 3.2--Consistent Attitude

At this sublevel, particular attitudes and preferences have become established parts of the individual's repertoire. He behaves in a particular way over and over again, and comes to feel that this reaction is correct and proper. The response has become ingrained through repetition and is now quite predictable. For the most part, the individual views his feelings and behaviors as natural, correct, and inherently good in their own right; however, when pressed, he may offer superficial supportive rationales in an off-hand manner.

Sublevel 3.3--Rationalized Attitude

At this sublevel, the individual comes to recognize the need to rationalize his attitudes, and begins to supply rationales in support of his responses to encountered ideas, notions, or situations. These rationales are not based on reflective thought, but rather they are supplied after the fact to support an attitudinal stance. The individual searches about, locates a reason that appears to be convenient or socially acceptable, and applies it to the situation. Thus, the individual is unconcerned about the worth of the rationale, other than that it should be acceptable to other people. There is no attempt to qualify or critically examine his thinking. For example, he may have grown up in a Democratic household and knows that he likes Democrats. When asked why, he may respond that "Roosevelt and the Democrats got us out of the Depression," simply because he heard it at home. Most people tend to operate predominately at sublevel 3.3-- Rationalized Attitude when engaged in their routine daily activities and pursuits.

LEVEL IV: VALIDATING

At some point in time, the individual begins to examine his conforming attitudes (and the rationales offered in their support), and determines whether or not he personally can believe in them. At this level of the model, he cognitively processes the attitudes.

That is, he examines them carefully in terms of alternatives and consequences, and ultimately accepts (or rejects) them for specific reasons.

Sublevel 4.1--Examining Values

At the lowest validating level, the individual detects that a rationale he has often used for an attitude needs to be examined for its merits. This act of cognitive examination has moved the individual's stance from a Conforming attitude to the sublevel 4.1--Examining Values. At this level, the individual carefully examines a possible value (and its rationale) from many angles in an effort to ascertain its acceptability. It is compared and contrasted with similar or alternative values and rationales (including those already accepted), and its consequences are made as explicit as possible. Ultimately, the value (with its alternatives and consequences considered) is related to his own experience, and becomes a candidate for acceptance or rejection.

Sublevel 4.2--Accepting Values

As this validation of values takes place, values and their rationales are decided upon and the individual "collects" a group of values. Any particular value can be defended, by itself, with some degree of assurance on the part of the individual. When a value reaches this stage, it is at sublevel 4.2--Accepting Values. At this level, the individual either accepts or rejects the value as important to his life; in short, it becomes a matter for personal commitment for specific reasons. The reasons (or rationale) offered in support of the decision may take either one (or a combination) of the following forms:

1. Consequential reasons (or rationale): where the value is deemed to lead to consequences which previously have been chosen as acceptable to the individual;

2. Criterial reasons (or rationale): where the value is analyzed as being consistent with criteria (or principles) which previously have been chosen as acceptable to the individual.

LEVEL V: AFFECTIVE JUDGING

The Affective Judging level includes two distinct but related types of value-related judgments. They are: (1) judgments related to the formulation of criteria that can serve as the basis for ordering and choosing between values, and (2) judgments related to the resolution of particular value conflicts.

Sublevel 5.1--Establishing Value Criteria

The process of examining and accepting or rejecting particular values takes place at the Validating level. As a result of this validating process, the individual becomes committed to a set of values (i.e., grounded beliefs) that influence his behavior in a variety of circumstances.

In the give-and-take of daily life the individual encounters situations and has experiences that prompt him to think about accepted values collectively. As a result of new experience, increasing value diversity, and the growing complexity of his value system, the individual is faced with the prospect of having to choose one value over another in certain situations. Hence, he begins to develop a set of value criteria that can be used as the basis for (1) ordering accepted values (setting priorities), (2) making choices between accepted values, and (3) screening new values. Thus, at sublevel 5.1--Establishing Value Criteria, the individual develops, internalizes, and makes explicit the principles or criterial base for ordering, choosing between, and screening values.

Once established, the value criteria will promote consistency and expedite the processing of values at the Validating level. But most importantly, in a particular situation the individual can now identify the relative importance of a given value to himself, and can explain why (using internalized value criteria) it is more or less important than related values. He is now prepared to deal with value conflict situations (i.e., value dilemmas) at the Value Judging sublevel. For example, a person who values both honesty and kindness may find himself in a situation where being honest with a very close friend will deeply hurt the friend's feelings. Thus, the individual is forced to

choose between honesty and kindness. In such value
conflict situations, the person's established value
criteria are brought into play as a guide in making
the value judgment.

Sublevel 5.2--Value Judging
(Criteria-based Decision
Resolving Value Conflict)

When an individual is confronted with a value conflict, he is in a position where he is forced to make
a decision (or choice) between two or more values of
importance to him. In dealing with such a dilemma at
the Value Judging sublevel, the individual will allow
varying degrees of cognition and previously established
value criteria to influence his decision.

When the individual makes use of his established
value criteria in rendering a value judgment he is
operating at sublevel 5.2--Value Judging. The value
conflict is "resolved" by a judgment based on the nature of his value criteria and the type of affective-
set that has evolved within his value system. If
asked, he can describe the principles or criteria upon
which the judgment is based.

LEVEL VI: AFFECTIVE CREATING

At the highest level of the affective domain the
individual is able to activate what has been termed the
creative imagination--essentially, the capacity to
visualize, to foresee, and to generate unique values.
The creative imagination functions in two ways. Initially it can be utilized to examine, probe, and explore the total value system. This process may reveal
relationships not previously apparent or recognized,
and consequently may lead to a reorganized and more
fully integrated value system. At a more sophisticated
level, the creative imagination can be utilized to
focus thought on ways of changing, altering, or reformulating the total value system. This process may result in unique insights about new values and new value
configurations. The functioning of the creative
imagination has been identified as the highest type of
human mental activity by many perceptive laymen and by
scholars involved in research in the field of creativity.[12] However, the creative imagination should not
be viewed as a phenomenon or activity unique to the

affective domain; it quite obviously operates across all three domains at the 6.0 level.

Sublevel 6.1--Integrating Values

When the individual is involved in the process of thinking about the meaning and organization of his total value system he is operating at sublevel 6.1-- Integrating Values. This involves relating, reassessing, and reformulating accepted values, established value criteria, and value judgments.

With respect to his accepted values, the individual relates new values to older values; older values are related to each other; and the new and the old are classified and reclassified with respect to their similarities, differences, consistencies, inconsistencies, and the types of circumstances in which they become activated. The individual is working toward developing a unique integrated system of values that is internally consistent, logical, and workable in the give-and-take of daily life.

With respect to his value criteria and value judgments, the individual may find that he is no longer satisfied with the value criteria he is using. At this point he may examine and revise his value criteria (i.e., return to sublevel 5.1 above) and render judgments about them. Thus, he becomes involved in a cycle of judgments using the value criteria, followed by interim judging and revising of the criteria. In such instances, the individual is actually examining and judging the mode of reasoning used in making judgments. He has come to reflect upon his choices and how they were arrived at; he can introspectively analyze and evaluate his own criteria (i.e., question their usefulness, examine alternative criteria, or ponder possible changes). Regardless of his present approach to value conflicts, he has now assumed a stance whereby he is willing to consider types of reasoning other than his own and may be able to develop and adopt broader, more flexible ways of viewing and dealing with values and value conflicts.

Sublevel 6.2--Inspirational Insight

The exact way in which creative insights are stimulated is somewhat obscure, but apparently it is related to encountered problems and/or feelings of dissonance and the consequent urge or desire to reflect upon the meaning(s) of experience (or existence) in a broad context with few constraints. The process may develop and proceed in the following manner. First, the individual perceives some kind of a "problem" relative to his value structure, and after considerable reflection about the functioning of his system of values he may seek out and examine alternative modes of valuing. This may prompt him to ponder the possibility of hybrid value systems containing elements of several systems in addition to his own. In turn, he may begin to think about unusual value formulations that are not directly related to any particular known system. Eventually, he may create or "discover" new value patterns or configurations that relate or encompass broad segments of human experience. (A variety of approaches has been suggested for triggering creative insights, including the metaphorical approach known as Synectics.)[13]

On occasion, after being involved in the process described above, the individual may experience a "flash of insight" that is totally (or largely) unique and apparently not a direct "spin-off" or a logical implication of any of his previous patterns of thought. In such instances, he has achieved what is herein termed sublevel 6.2--Inspirational Insight.

For centuries many Eastern religious and philosophical systems have emphasized special techniques and disciplines designed to promote Inspirational Insights. The disciplines of Yoga and Zen Buddhism are two well-known examples. Many similar but less rigorous "mind expanding" techniques have been advocated in recent years.[14] Throughout history many creative, intuitive, and unique insights, with obvious affective overtones and value orientations, have been attributed to moral and religious philosophers, to social theorists, and to many influential but less well-known individuals. For example, in the realm of religion and moral philosophy, apparent inspirational insights are associated with Gautama Buddha, Lao-tzu, and Mohammed. In the more secular realms, the names of theorists such as Plato, Descartes, and Gandhi come to mind. It should be noted, however, that in most instances of insight the cognitive and affective components are intimately related and merged together in such a way as to be almost inseparable.

SUMMARY OF LEVELS IN THE
AFFECTIVE DOMAIN

I. AFFECTIVE PERCEIVING

    1.1 Emotive Imprinting

    1.2 Response Setting

II. REACTING

    2.1 Emoting

    2.2 Recognizing

    2.3 Controlling

III. CONFORMING

    3.1 Artificial Attitude

    3.2 Consistent Attitude

    3.3 Rationalized Attitude

IV. VALIDATING (Processing Values)

    4.1 Examining Values

    4.2 Accepting Values

V. AFFECTIVE JUDGING

    5.1 Establishing Value Criteria

    5.2 Value Judging (Criteria-based Decision
        Resolving Value Conflict)

VI. AFFECTIVE CREATING

    6.1 Integrating Values

    6.2 Inspirational Insight

ENDNOTES

[1] These four approaches are adapted from discussions in the following references: Harry S. Broudy, B. Othanel Smith, and Joe R. Burnett, Democracy and Excellence in American Secondary Education (Chicago: Rand McNally, 1964), pp. 139-41; and Maurice P. Hunt and Lawrence E. Metcalf, Teaching High School Social Studies (New York: Harper and Row, Publishers, 1968), pp. 121-23.

[2] For further discussions of these ideas, see also Prescott Lecky, Self Consistency: A Theory of Personality (New York: Island Press, 1945).

[3] For a detailed discussion of the conclusions presented in this section, see Charles E. Gray, "Value Education Outcomes: Implications for the Social Studies Methods Course," Unpublished doctoral dissertation, University of Illinois, 1968.

[4] W. F. Ogburn, Social Change (New York: Viking Press, 1922); and William O. Stanley, Education and Social Integration (New York: Teachers College, Columbia University, 1953).

[5] Guilford discusses a variety of relationships between his model and other traits of personality in J. P. Guilford, The Analysis of Intelligence (New York: McGraw-Hill Book Company, 1971), pp. 279-345.

[6] Louis E. Raths, Merrill Harmin, and Sidney B. Simon, Values and Teaching (Columbus, Ohio: Charles E. Merrill, 1966), pp. 27-33.

[7] Abraham Maslow, "Psychological Data and Value Theory," in New Knowledge in Human Values, ed. Abraham Maslow (New York: Harper and Row, Publishers, 1959), p. 123.

[8] For a further discussion of the Maslow hierarchy, see the following: Abraham Maslow, Motivation and Personality (New York: Harper and Row, Publishers, 1954 and 1970); and Abraham Maslow, "A Theory of Human Motivation," Psychological Review, 50 (1943):270-96.

[9] Harry S. Broudy, _Building a Philosophy of Education_, 2d ed. (Englewood Cliffs, New Jersey: Prentice-Hall, Inc., 1961), pp. 125-26, 172.

[10] Ibid., pp. 141-43.

[11] D. R. Krathwohl, B. S. Bloom, and B. B. Masia, _Taxonomy of Educational Objectives, Handbook II: Affective Domain_ (New York: David McKay, Inc., 1964), pp. 176-85.

[12] Alex F. Osborn, _Applied Imagination_ (New York: Charles Scribner's Sons, 1963), Chapters One and Two; and William J. J. Gordon, _Synectics_ (New York: Harper and Row, Publishers, 1961), Chapter One.

[13] Gordon, _Synectics_, Chapter Two.

[14] For example, two articles dealing with Transcendental Meditation appeared in the December 1972 issue of the _Phi Delta Kappan_, a highly respected educational journal.

CHAPTER IV--Physical Endeavors:
The Prince of the Domains

Just as with the affective and cognitive domains, various schemes have been developed for classifying objectives in the psychomotor domain. Inconsistent sorting factors have rendered some such classificatory systems difficult to use. Certain systems have confined themselves to muscular coordination only, thereby permitting only minimum application for most practicing teachers.

A REVIEW OF PSYCHOMOTOR CLASSIFICATIONS

RAGSDALE

In 1950 Ragsdale assembled a classification of psychomotor relationships to learning behaviors.[1] Ragsdale pointed out that every content area contains elements of the psychomotor domain, and therefore structured his three-part psychomotor classification system so as to highlight those relationships.

According to Ragsdale, when individuals are manipulating or dealing with an object, their psychomotor involvement is labeled Object-Motor activity. In another category, Language-Motor, all movements that deal with speech, handwriting, or other construction or interpretation of symbols are categorized. When an individual is relating to attitudes, feelings, and emotions through movement, then Ragsdale labels the relationship <u>Feeling</u>-<u>Motor</u>.

As can be seen, Ragsdale made use of the three domains. When one deals with movements that reflect high cognition through language, they are classified as <u>Language</u>-<u>Motor</u>. If the movement is an outgrowth of the affective domain, it is called <u>Feeling</u>-<u>Motor</u>. If the emphasis is on psychomotor execution movement, it is called <u>Object</u>-<u>Motor</u>.

SIMPSON

A seven-level psychomotor scheme was developed by Simpson in 1966.[2] In some critiques, reviewers have confined themselves to its first five levels. These are 1.0 <u>Perception</u>, defined as an awareness by way of sensory input; 2.0 <u>Set</u>, a mental, physical, and emotional readiness to perform; 3.0 <u>Guided Response</u>, dealing with modeling behavior and guidance during performance; 4.0 <u>Mechanism</u>, allowing for the execution of skills and habituation of performances; and 5.0 <u>Complex Overt Response</u>, which encompasses the execution of complex patterns of movement. At this point, Simpson adds two more important levels that psychomotor purists may reject because they see elements of cognition. These are 6.0 <u>Adaptation</u>, which allows for modifications in movement, and 7.0 <u>Originations</u>, which allow for creativity in movement.

KIBLER, BARKER, AND MILES

Another model for classification within the psychomotor domain was suggested by Kibler, Barker, and Miles in 1970.[3] Not intended to be taxonomical, their scheme involved four areas. The first of these is 1.0 <u>Gross Bodily Movements</u>, in which there are movements of limbs coordinated with body parts or the limbs themselves. In area 2.0, <u>Finely Coordinated Movements</u> are classified as movements in patterns or sequences of the extremities. When an individual is attempting to convey a message without words, he is operating in area 3.0 <u>Non-Verbal</u> Communication Behavior. When involved in communication activities, the individual is operating in the 4.0 <u>Speech Behaviors</u> area.

In this scheme, Kibler, et al. have many subcategories which often allow for overlap. For instance, if the individual is combining speech (4.0) with facial expression and gestures (3.0), then the combination is classified at 4.4 <u>Sound</u>-<u>Gesture</u> <u>Coordination</u>.

HAUENSTEIN

A. Dean Hauenstein suggested a psychomotor domain classification scheme that allows elements of the affective and cognitive domains to infiltrate.4 Obviously intended to be practical, the scheme involves five levels (without sublevels). At level 1, Hauenstein has paralleled the work of Simpson and used the label <u>Perception</u>, intending essentially the same meaning. At level 2, he has used the label <u>Imitation</u>. This level is very close to Simpson's level 3.0 <u>Guided</u> <u>Response</u>, in which the individual is duplicating a behavior in response to external stimuli. When an individual is using skills that he has developed through imitation in an analagous situation, Hauenstein classifies that use at his third level, <u>Manipulation</u>. At the fourth and fifth levels, <u>Performance</u> and <u>Perfection</u>, the individual uses more cognition and improves his psychomotor skill ability.

HARROW

A complex attempt at classifying psychomotor domain behaviors, which includes many sublevels, is that of Anita Harrow.5 Harrow emphasizes that her taxonomic classification is of "behaviors unique to the psychomotor domain."6 Thus it is most useful as an aid to "educators and curriculum developers to classify and categorize relevant movement experiences for children."7 The six levels in this scheme are as follows:

1.0 <u>Reflex</u> <u>Movements</u>--Involuntary movements essential as a psychomotor base;

2.0 <u>Basic</u>-<u>Fundamental</u> <u>Movements</u>--Motor patterns based upon reflex movements which emerge without training;

3.0 <u>Perceptual</u> <u>Abilities</u>--Includes all sensory input to the brain;

4.0 Physical Abilities--Includes the elements necessary for the development of proficient movement which "if not adequately developed can be limiting factors to the development of highly skilled movement";[8]

5.0 Skilled Movements--As an individual builds movement skills, they can be classified as simple, compound, and complex. Each of these can be further categorized as beginner, intermediate, advanced or highly skilled; and

6.0 Non-Discursive Communication--Encompasses behaviors in which all attempts to communicate through movement are classified.

CONCLUSIONS REGARDING PSYCHOMOTOR CLASSIFICATION SCHEMES

Upon examination, it becomes apparent that the practicing teacher has been offered several psychomotor schemes, any of which may include one of the following problems. First, the sorting factors for classifying are allowed to shift. Second, some schemes are so complex they are unlikely to be used. Third, even though some schemes can be used, they are of limited value to practicing teachers because objectives derived from them will not reflect the relationship of the psychomotor domain to the other domains. Lastly, because the schemes do not present an analogous relationship between the domains, the teacher must work with a fresh category system for each domain, learning and working with it as an entity in itself. In the real world, this added dimension is likely to leave the scheme unused.

THE PIERCE-GRAY CLASSIFICATION MODEL FOR THE PSYCHOMOTOR DOMAIN

Psychomotor classification systems seldom distinguish between sensory inputs, mental processing, and outputs. By contrast, the classification model herein proposed recognizes the distinction between sensory inputs to the brain, the cognitive and/or affective processing of the inputs, and the consequent

66

transmission of the outputs (in the form of "instructions" to physical body machinery). Once the above distinctions and relationships are made explicit, the degree of cognition emerges as the pervasive psychomotor sorting factor (as was the case for the affective domain). Thus, a scheme which employs increments of cognition as the basis for classification should be useful to the practitioner. What follows is a description of a psychomotor classification model that utilizes the degree of cognition as the basic sorting factor.

LEVEL I: PSYCHOMOTOR PERCEIVING

Sublevel 1.1--Sensory Transmission

The fundamental physical process of the human body is the transmission of data through the sensory channels to the central nervous system. This is accomplished when the senses activate nerve channels that carry signals (or "messages"). Signals related to hereditary body functions are automatically routed to the autonomic (involuntary) nervous system where they are routinely processed. Other signals are routed to the control centers of the cerebrum where they may be processed through the voluntary system. This transmission process is labeled, sublevel 1.1--Sensory Transmission.

When a signal (message) reaches the cerebrum, the brain performs the functions described at 1.1 and 1.2 in the cognitive and affective domains. In addition, the capacity for output (Physical Action Potential) is developed.

Sublevel 1.2--Physiofunctional Maintenance

The capacity to move the body and any of its parts is complicated by the interactions and complimentary blending of functions of the autonomic and voluntary systems. The voluntary system is controlled by thought, and voluntary movements are activated by both hemispheres of the cerebrum. The autonomic system controls involuntary body functions and is a product of the individual's hereditary set and genetic package. Through practice, certain individuals have

67

been known to gain control over portions of the autonomic system (i.e., being able to control heartbeat
rates), but usually creation of the Physical Action
Potential is simply the brain's storing of capacities
to activate body machinery.

In relation to these functions, the body's autonomic system is continuously performing a maintenance
function in order to ensure its physical storage and
output potentials. This includes not only regular
maintenance functions such as breathing and processing
of food, but also keeping the brain and its cognitive
and affective action potentials in readiness.

Hence, for this classification model, sublevel
1.2--Physiofunctional Maintenance includes the storing
and maintenance functions described above.

LEVEL II: ACTIVATING

As an infant develops in muscular control and
coordination, various parts of the body become more
and more skilled in movement. The psychomotor domain
is simply the development of basic physical and sensing skills with gradual increases in cognition. For
reasons related to sex, geographic location, parental
interest, cultural pressure, and so on, individuals
develop various degrees or levels of physical coordination.

Three principles are associated with the normal
growth cycle of development. The first is called the
cephalocaudal principle. It simply means that growth
and motor development proceed generally from the head
to the tail of the organism. The second is called
the proximodistal principle. This principle states
that growth and motor development proceed from the
axis of the body outward. Gross body movements are
gradually replaced by fine body movements. The third
principle is that of motor chaining. The individual
becomes more efficient in any motor activity he practices (and it becomes more automatic). Those muscle
sequences that are not helpful drop out, and those
that are helpful remain and become more and more useful.

Most basic motor coordinating has been accomplished before the child enters school. Objectives

68

at the Activating level often take the form of norms.
For instance, by age eight months most infants are
crawling. Occasionally a primary teacher may discover
that some basic motor skill needs attention. An objective for this particular child may then be in
order. As Harrow puts it,

> It should be obvious that when the "stan-
> dard model" walks through the kindergarten
> doorway he should have with him a basic
> reflex system which has given way to a
> well-developed motor system manifested
> through a variety of controlled locomotor,
> non-locomotor, and manipulative movements.
> His perceptual abilities, which have been
> developing through maturation and learning
> since the first four weeks of life when he
> began his initial practices, utilizing his
> visual, auditory, and kinesthetic modali-
> ties, are ready for further sophistication.
> Occasionally the "model" or learner who
> walks through the door to formal education
> does not have all the essential "equipment,"
> and therefore must have an individualized
> program developed to assist him in obtain-
> ing all the prerequisites to efficient func-
> tioning of the psychomotor as well as the
> cognitive and affective domains of learning.[9]

Sublevel 2.1--Physical Outputs

At the initial stages of Activating, the capacities for body movement are put into motion. A differentiation again must be made between those body
machinery efforts that are a product of the autonomic
system, as opposed to the first attempts made by the
organism as a result of conscious voluntary action.

Sublevel 2.2--Mimicry

At sublevel 2.2--Mimicry, the individual simply
engaged in modeling behavior after observing the
movements of another. There is not a conscious
effort to make the Mimicry precisely that of the imi-
tated, and there is little thought of retaining the
skill in a permanent skill repertoire. It is a moment
of effort to produce peculiar body effects; it probably
will not be practiced much, and little effort will be

69

made to move it toward the automatic level.

Sublevel 2.3--Deliberate Modeling

If, however, there is an attempt to practice for
retention, and thought is given to making the imitation as close as possible to that of the demonstration,
then the individual has moved to sublevel 2.3--Delib-
erate Modeling. The modeling is conscious and meaningful to the individual. The individual has begun
an attempt to develop what is labeled "muscle memory."
The skill is one which the individual wishes to be
able to "call-up" at any time.

LEVEL III: EXECUTING

When a particular psychomotor skill can be performed to accomplish an understood task without
further practice, then the individual has reached the
Executing level. When presented with a set of circumstances that demand the use of particular skills,
those skills can be executed to complete the task.
The typist can insert paper and type the necessary
copy. The basketball player can attempt the free
throw. The scientist can manipulate the controls of
the microscope. The individual is aware of the
necessary skills required and initiates the appropriate motor responses. He can explain the procedure
that he is following in his Execution.

Sublevel 3.1--Task Execution

At sublevel 3.1--Task Execution, the individual
engages in the appropriate skill automatically. He
understands why he is so engaged and for what ultimate
purpose, but little cognition is required in the actual
Execution. For instance, at this level the individual
may simply engage in the act of feeding himself,
skillfully using all of the table equipments. Entire
meals may be eaten without cognition about the act of
eating, but cognition can be activated if necessary.

Sublevel 3.2--Operational Execution

When cognition must accompany the skill or skills
in their accomplishment periodically, then the

individual is operating at sublevel 3.2--Operational Execution. At this level much of the Execution is automatic, but cognition is necessary at intervals. For instance, in the act of driving a car, much of the Execution can be done with little cognitive concentration. Periodically, however, cognition in directing the executive skills is crucial.

Sublevel 3.3--Skilled Execution

On occasion the individual may find it necessary to concentrate on the Execution of skills cognitively a high per cent of the time. This would be true of the surgeon in an operation or the golfer Executing a shot. Loss of concentration could cost a life or a stroke. When the individual is so engaged, he is operating at sublevel 3.3--Skilled Execution. It is obvious that the highly skilled professional athlete exhibits this level of Execution a high percentage of the time.

LEVEL IV: MANEUVERING

At this level the individual must make decisions as to what skills to use in given situations. The individual may try an approach to see if a particular learned skill can be Executed to accomplish a desired end. If not, another approach may be substituted. Similarities and differences between the current situation and other situations in the past are considered as an aid in making the decision.

Sublevel 4.1--Inspecting Skills

In the process of Executing skills, the individual often discovers that others have been able to reach a higher skill level. Also, he may surmise that if certain skills are altered or replaced, his own efficiency at certain tasks may be improved. In this examination of skills, he compares his skills with others and begins to deduce optimal skill arrangements for particular sets of circumstances. For instance, when the basketball player dribbles down the court with an opponent between himself and a teammate who is under the basket, he may choose to execute a bounce, chest, baseball, lob, or other pass. By comparing this set of circumstances with others he has encountered, he is engaging in skill inspection.

Sublevel 4.2--Selecting Skills

Closely related to the inspection process is the periodic trial and selection of specific skills or sets of skills. As improvements are made, certain of the trials that are being inspected are adopted. In actual practice, the entire process may involve moving down one or more levels where a new skill (or skills) is modeled and practiced until successfully executed. Thereupon, the skill(s) undergoes repeated trials where it is carefully inspected, refined, and/or revised. Ultimately, the process of selection culminates in the rejection or acceptance of the skill(s). For instance, a professional baseball pitcher who is successful on the basis of a "slider" and "fast" ball may at the same time be working to bring his "curve" and "fork" ball past the deliberate modeling stage, through skilled execution to inspection for possible adoption, and on to final selection (or rejection). An implication is that this skill selection leads to an analytical conclusion that is a best answer upon which all professional ball players would agree.

LEVEL V: PSYCHOMOTOR JUDGING

Skill judging involves considerably more cognition than the lower levels. Indeed, it is possible that in some circumstances actual psychomotor acts may be absent for the individual making the judgment. That is, he may be judging acts engaged in by other people. Whether individuals can make accurate judgments about their own skills while engaged in their execution is a moot point. Even the finest professional golfers will take their swings to another pro for assistance in making judgments.

When operating at sublevel 4.2--Selecting Skills, where the "right" answer is sought, circumstances may occur in which there is not an answer to which the logic of the situation leads. At this moment in time, the individual working with the skills must render a judgment, based on evidence. Because of the number of variables, differences of opinion between people will exist.

Sublevel 5.1--Establishing Performance Criteria

Before rendering a judgment about which skill to use or how to use a performance skill, the individual must first assemble, analyze, and render an opinion about the criteria he will use to make the performance judgment. In some instances the criteria are already partially structured for the individual. For instance, at a diving competition, each judge has seen many dives and the criteria used in judging dives have been discussed, argued over, and written about. Still, the judge has a slightly different conceptual model of the "ideal" dive, and when assigning a score, the criteria he uses will be slightly different than each of the other judges. On occasion (as in the Olympics), the criteria may include other special considerations (such as the country represented) that will dramatically alter an assigned score.

In other situations, a machinist must make his own complete set of criteria for judging which of his psychomotor skills to bring into play in order to produce a given product. He may choose to use a band saw, shaper, and surface grinder rather than a radial saw and mill, because his own psychomotor ability with each has been used as one of the judgmental criteria.

Sublevel 5.2--Performance Judging (Criteria-based Decision from Alternatives)

Once the performance criteria have been established, the final judgment or series of Performance Judgments can take place. The individual attempts to make skill assessments (judgments) using his own criteria. A coach attempting to assist the baseball hitter assesses the swing against a conceptualized model of the ideal swing.

LEVEL VI: PSYCHOMOTOR CREATING

Sublevel 6.1--Combining Skills

Often the criteria established and judgments rendered are operationalized because of a desire to build or construct a new product. The pieces may be put together in a variety of ways, but using analytical skills and developed criteria and judgments, the skills are combined to create a new whole. For instance, the football coach may watch game films of future opponents and form opinions of their capabilities. He also is constantly appraising his own players and their effects upon each other. On the basis of these assessments, he may then begin the formulation of game plans. The effectiveness of his game plans is directly related to the validity of a series of interrelated judgments. Ultimately the individual may allow himself to approach the problem of judging solutions by creating an environment in which highly imaginative solutions to skill problems are discovered. Should such a solution emerge, sublevel 6.2--Performance Insight will have occurred.

When John McKay created the "I" formation for football, when the first baseball coach used the Ted Williams shift, when Willie Shoemaker rides an unexpected winner, who can really attest to whether the adjusted skills were a product of judgment or insight?

SUMMARY OF LEVELS IN THE
PSYCHOMOTOR DOMAIN

I. PSYCHOMOTOR PERCEIVING

    1.1 Sensory Transmission

    1.2 Physiofunctional Maintenance

II. ACTIVATING

    2.1 Physical Outputs

    2.2 Mimicry

    2.3 Deliberate Modeling

III. EXECUTING

    3.1 Task Execution

    3.2 Operational Execution

    3.3 Skilled Execution

IV. MANEUVERING

    4.1 Inspecting Skills

    4.2 Selecting Skills

V. PSYCHOMOTOR JUDGING

    5.1 Establishing Performance Criteria

    5.2 Performance Judging (Criteria-based Decision from Alternatives)

VI. PSYCHOMOTOR CREATING

    6.1 Combining Skills

    6.2 Performance Insight

ENDNOTES

[1]C. E. Ragsdale, "How Children Learn Motor Types of Activities," Learning and Instruction, Forty-ninth Yearbook of the National Society for the Study of Education (Chicago: University of Chicago Press, 1950), pp. 69-71.

[2]E. J. Simpson, The Classification of Educational Objectives: Psychomotor Domain (Urbana: University of Illinois Press, 1966), pp. 68-104.

[3]R. J. Kibler, L. L. Barker, and D. T. Miles, Behavioral Objectives and Instruction (Boston: Allyn and Bacon, Inc., 1970), pp. 68-75.

[4]A. Dean Hauenstein, Curriculum Planning for Behavioral Development (Worthington, Ohio: Charles A. Jones Publishing Company, 1972), pp. 19-22.

[5]A. J. Harrow, A Taxonomy of the Psychomotor Domain (New York: David McKay Inc., 1972).

[6]Ibid., p. 1.

[7]Ibid.

[8]Ibid., p. 69.

[9]Ibid., pp. 43-44.

CHAPTER V--Strategies in the Use of the Cognitive Domain

There is little doubt that traditionally the primary focus (and effort) of formal education has been oriented toward the cognitive domain. This has resulted in the development of a wide variety of approaches, views, and philosophical positions regarding how to teach, what should be emphasized, and what content should be taught. This chapter will examine several ways in which the classification model for the cognitive domain may be applied. It also will analyze a number of teaching-learning strategies in terms of the intellectual levels involved when they are used in the classroom.

CORRESPONDENCE BETWEEN OBJECTIVES, LEARNING ACTIVITIES, AND EVALUATIONS

Several reasons exist for the lack of correspondence often found between learning activities and evaluations in classrooms. One reason is the pressure felt by many teachers to arrange the students in each class into a "curve" of grades. By teaching at one level and testing at another, the teacher is more likely to have a "spread" of scores, and hence be able to assign a variety of marks. A second reason, shamefully, is that the teacher simply does not realize that he is shifting cognitive levels. The following examples will serve to illustrate this point.

Most students at one time or another experience a teaching-learning situation in which the course is primarily designed around a series of lectures. The teacher talks and the students listen. The students may or may not be permitted to ask questions during or after the lecture to clarify points or concepts. The intellectual level of the learning activity in this course is "Understanding"[1] within the classification model. Therefore, the implied evaluation level for the course is also "Understanding." The students anticipate--and rightly so--that they should be remembering facts, concepts, and relationships, and will be expected to explain, describe, or otherwise indicate their accrued Understandings.

Quite often, however, the students will encounter an evaluation instrument that asks them to use the skills of Applying, Analyzing, Judging, and Creating in dealing with the information which has been presented in the class. When this happens, the teacher has begun to administer something more akin to an intelligence test than a valid achievement test. Assuming that all students had studied and Understood the material presented, the student with the greater intellectual ability would score highest if the teacher constructed a test requiring primarily the demonstration of several higher order cognitive skills. There is some empirical evidence to support this notion.[2]

A similar, but reversed situation, is also often encountered. In the classroom the teacher leads a series of discussions based on reading assignments. During the discussions the students are bombarded with many probing, penetrating questions. No student's statements are safe from the scrutiny of the instructor. But the test turns out to be a series of two hundred true and false questions that assess the students' ability to Understand the content covered in the readings.

Along with the problems of low correspondence between learning activities and evaluations, there also exists a difficulty often encountered between objectives and evaluations. Unfortunately, teachers do not convey precise objectives to students much of the time. But even with those who do, there is a tendency to indicate what the students will be expected to do in the objective, but then evaluate them on something else. For instance, if the teacher indicates that students will be able to "identify the similarities and differences between Russian Communism and Chinese Communism," but then asks students to "choose whether they would rather live under Russian Communism or Chinese Communism, and supply at least five reasons for their choice," the students have been told they will be tested at the Analysis level, but they actually are being asked to operate at the Cognitive Judging level during the evaluation.

The teacher who wishes to ensure that there is a correspondence between objectives, learning activities, and evaluations can make use of the cognitive classification model to identify the cognitive levels for each. When all three of these aspects of the educational enterprise are at the same level, learning will be enhanced.

ENSURING A CROSS-SECTION OF INTELLECTUAL ENDEAVORS

A charge often leveled at the educational community is that there is too much emphasis at the lower cognitive levels. Unfortunately, this may well be true. In many content areas, academic leaders do not question the intellectual levels at which their content is taught. For instance, mathematics teachers may well be satisfied if they can get students to understand rules and use them to solve numerical problems. Developing analysis skills, such as selecting the proper formulas to solve word problems, often receives less attention in mathematics classrooms.

In other content areas, similar situations emerge. For instance, instead of developing higher-level skills to analyze data, generate hypotheses, or evaluate notions, teachers often simply increase the complexity of the concepts taught. By making the concepts more involved, the teacher often feels that the intellectual level has been raised. This, however, is not necessarily true. What has happened is that the teacher has simply made the instructional planning task more intricate. The teaching strategy in explaining the concept must be more carefully arranged to lead the students in a step-by-step fashion to ensure Understanding.

Often even a casual inspection of objectives and learning activities will reveal that one or another

level is receiving an inordinate amount of emphasis.
By consistently checking the intellectual levels, and
with revised planning, an improved balance among
intellectual levels can be attained.

USING THE CLASSIFICATION MODEL
IN PLANNING

The cognitive classification model may be used
as a device in planning for the selection and development of skills in the teaching of particular content.
A logical approach for deciding on the cognitive
skills counterpart to content would include first, the
identification of objectives at the Understanding
level, and second, listing objectives at succeeding
levels.

For instance, assume that election procedures is
the content topic. The teacher begins by identifying
the material that must be Understood; and then asks
himself, "What concepts, facts, and relationships
should the student be able to describe and explain?"
From this question objectives such as, "The student
will be able to explain the section of Roberts' Rules
of Order dealing with elections" are generated (Understanding). Next, the teacher asks, "What rules or
principles have been learned that could be Applied?"
The answer to this question leads to the generation of
objectives such as, "The students will be able to
elect class officers following the procedures outlined
in Roberts' Rules of Order" (Applying).

Continuing to ask appropriate questions at each
subsequent level, the teacher can develop objectives
for Analyzing, Judging, and Creating based upon the
same content theme.

Analyzing--"The student will be able to identify
from documents at least four similarities and four
differences between the Roberts' Rules of Order election procedures and the election process used by the
U.S. House of Representatives."

Cognitive Judging--"Given an election situation
and three possible election procedures, the students
will be able to judge which of the three they believe
to be best, and present at least four logical or
empirical rationales for their judgment."

<u>Cognitive Creating</u>--"When presented with a hypo-
thetical election situation, the student will be able
to produce an original set of election procedures
that would be useable in that circumstance."

An Example of the
Model for History

Topic: World War II--Battle Strategies

<u>Understanding</u>------The student will be able to
describe the basic strategy
used by Rommel in his North
African campaign.

<u>Applying</u>----------Given a previously unseen bat-
tle situation, the student will
use the principles developed by
Rommel to simulate a battle on
a scale-model terrain.

<u>Analyzing</u>----------Provided with five battle
strategies, never before seen,
the student will label each as
to the general who utilized
the strategy style.

<u>Cognitive Judging</u>--Given a complete hypothetical
military situation and five
possible battle strategies, the
student will evaluate each and
render a judgment as to the one
which he believes most likely
to be successful, supplying a
series of reasons for his
judgment.

<u>Cognitive Creating</u>-After reviewing a set of data
about enemy forces, their
habits, equipment, terrain, and
movements, the student will
develop an original battle
strategy for that situation.

Topic: Science Fiction

Understanding------The student will be able to explain five basic elements that
are unique to creating a
science fiction tale.

Analyzing---------Given a short science fiction
story, the student will be
able to identify each of five
basic elements (or lack there-
of) within that short story.

Cognitive Judging--When presented with three
science fiction stories, the
student will be able to judge
which of them makes the best
use of the five elements unique
to science fiction, and support
the judgment with examples and
illustrations from the provided
short stories.

Cognitive Creating-The student will be able to
outline an original short
science fiction plot that contains the five basic elements
unique to science fiction.

An Example of the Model
for Industrial Arts-Woods

Topic: Joints

Understanding------The student will be able to
describe at least four types of
wood joints used in furniture
making.

Applying----------The student will follow a step-
by-step set of instructions to
assemble four types of pre-cut
model wood joints.

Analyzing----------Given a series of pictures of
previously unseen furniture,
the student will be able to
classify each according to the
style of joints commonly used
for that type of furniture.

Cognitive Judging--Given a design for an item of
furniture, complete except for
joints, the student will
select the joints he determines to be best for the
furniture item. If asked, the
student will be able to supply
a logical defense, with supportive data, for the choices
he made.

Cognitive Creating-The student will be able to
design an original piece of
furniture that uses at least
three different types of
joints.

As can be seen from the examples provided, any
topic from a content area can be viewed in terms of
skill development from level to level within the cognitive domain. The classification model serves as a
guide for the creation of a variety of objectives if
the teacher moves progressively to a higher level for
each new objective.

At this point, the highest level referred to in
planning is Cognitive Creating: 6.1--Uniting Ideas.
It is possible that within the framework of these
assignments, the student could operate at the 6.2--
Creative Insight level. This possibility exists, although all the teacher can do is allow, or set the
stage, for the possibility. That is, a conducive environment for Creative Insights can be structured as
part of the instructional activities, but an actual
outcome of 6.2--Creative Insights may or may not take
place.

COGNITIVE LEVELS USED IN SELECTED
TEACHING STRATEGIES

EXPOSITION

Exposition is defined here as all forms of teaching in which knowledge is explained, defined, and demonstrated to students. There are many ways to transmit knowledge from one person to another. Several approaches are explored below along with an analysis of the cognitive levels associated with each teaching approach or procedure.

The Lecture

As alluded to earlier, the basic cognitive level implied by the lecture is Understanding. The data that the teacher wishes to be transmitted are being moved from the mind of the teacher to the mind of the student through talking and listening. There is little chance for an Application of that data to take place during the lecture. It is possible that the student may be able to see similarities between the data being received and other experiences, thus involving the student in a degree of Analysis. Similarly, the data could be Judged or links identified to Create a new concept or conclusion. If these processes are used, however, it is strictly up to the student, and incidental to the instructional intent implied by the lecture.

The lecturer, if intellectually active within the field, is likely to have engaged in Analyzing and Judging the content being covered. The lecture platform provides an opportunity for the teacher to share the results of his own Analyzing and Judging and to hold the student responsible for Understanding them.

The Demonstration

Admittedly, there are many types and styles of demonstration; the distinct difference between a demonstration and a lecture is the intention of the instructor. Whereas the lecture does not imply any specific use of the data or concepts presented other than their regurgitation, the demonstration implies a move from the Understanding level to the Applying level (sometimes with a Psychomotor Domain Modeling behavior accompanying the Application).

In mathematics classes, for instance, the teacher demonstrates how a new type of problem can be solved. At the elementary level, this might reflect the objective, "The student will be able to compute the remainders of two-digit subtraction problems in which the one's place in the subtrahend is larger than the one's place in the minuend." The teacher models the technique at the chalkboard in a demonstration until the students Understand the principles involved. Then the students Apply the principles learned on assigned problems, assisted by the teacher when individuals encounter difficulty. Often the students are then given drill problems for homework in which they Apply the skill repeatedly until it is overlearned. Thus it is hoped that the skill will be instilled in the student and a new skill, built upon the old, may then be introduced.

In other areas, demonstrations are often used in a laboratory environment. Business machines, cooking, metals, physical education, and drafting are a few of the areas where the demonstration is a crucial part of the teaching methodology. The basic levels implied in the demonstration are Understanding and Applying. If the student goes beyond this to individually discover connections with other learning, or engages in a Value Judging process, it is beyond the level ordinarily planned by the teacher, and a matter of serendipity.

Instructional Media

The use of instructional media is limited to the transmission of content, and therefore is classified as an instructional device for the Understanding level. The intriguing thing about media is that when combined with other teaching techniques, especially discussion, media may become an excellent springboard for movement to higher levels within the cognitive classification model. Since media can present a varied accounting of all types of reality, reactions of thought about content presented are easily produced through media. Comparing and contrasting, making judgments, and generating hypotheses are all stimulated through the use of media.

Although seldom stated so directly, one of the central messages of many audio-visual college courses taught for the benefit of pre-service and in-service teachers, is an appeal to use media in a way that inspires thought rather than as a procedure to transmit knowledge alone. The crucial element is not the use of media itself, it is the manner in which the teacher utilizes it so as to stimulate _practice_ in higher-order thought within the students' minds.

SELF-INSTRUCTIONAL MATERIALS

There are numerous procedures currently in use that include the notion of self-pacing. Among these are computer assisted instruction, programmed materials based on reading, and self-instructional packages. In each case, materials can be produced at a variety of cognitive levels, but the type of procedure chosen implies a particular cognitive level or levels. When the builder of the materials attempts to violate the optimum level for the learning procedure, its effectiveness is diminished. This does not mean that a particular approach cannot be stretched to a higher level (or lowered) and be effective. It simply means that the most efficient procedure has not been used.

Readings

One of the oldest teaching techniques is assigned readings. By themselves, readings transmit content and function best for learning at the Understanding level. It is possible, however, to direct the student through higher-level thought through reading. For instance, at the Application level it is possible to describe the procedure for assembling a bicycle through reading. Anyone who has attempted to follow such directions, however, will attest to the fact that as a teaching technique there are better ways to learn to assemble bicycles.

Computer-assisted Instruction

There are a variety of styles of teaching programs utilizing the computer. The more sophisticated of these allows an interaction between student and machine. Thus, incorrect responses cause the computer

86

to cycle the student through proper remedial exercises, thus tailoring the instruction to specific needs.

Computer-assisted instruction has been most successful through the Applying level and in some forms of simple Analyzing, mainly classification. The computer can assist the student in developing the necessary rules and principles, and then engage him in Applying those rules and principles in practice exercises. In classification, the student learns the characteristics of certain categories, then previously unencountered examples are presented to be sorted. It is also possible to develop programs in which the student engages in concept learning through examples (see "Discovery Learning" below) prior to classification.

Because most computer programs classify responses as "right" or "wrong," their use is limited at the Evaluating and Creating levels.

Linear Reading Programs

Linear reading programs attempt to present concepts in very small increments with enough repetition so that no branching is needed. Since its very nature is reading, the most successful level of cognitive operation is Understanding. Many such programs have been written at higher levels, however. What is interesting about such programs is that for the right student they can be more expedient than regular classroom instruction. This is because the student is not slowed by the pace of the class. Because of this, some program advocates have felt that the linear program offers the most expedient teaching procedure for certain content areas and particular types of students. It is more likely, however, that for such exceptional students the ideal teaching procedure is instruction on a one-to-one (teacher-pupil) basis. This, however, is not presently possible in most school situations.

Self-instructional Packages

Self-instructional packages are variously named, such as Learning Activity Packages, Learning Modules, Self-instructional Modules, Individually Prescribed Modules, plus a host of other commercial and privately coined rubrics. What all of the quality packages have

in common are (1) a behaviorally stated objective
describing what the student is to be able to do upon
completion of the package, (2) a pre-assessment procedure to determine the initial status of the learners
in relation to the objective, (3) a set of learning
activities to assist the student in accomplishing the
objective, and (4) an evaluation procedure to verify
that the competency called for in the objective has
been attained by the student. If one of these four
elements is omitted, it is most usually the pre-
assessment procedure. In many cases, package builders
include a variety of additional sections, such as
enrichment activities, materials needed, trial tests
to be taken by the student prior to final evaluation,
estimates of time needed to complete the package, and
alternative learning activities.

In self-instructional packages, the key to determining the cognitive classification level is the objective. Since the learning activities within self-
instructional packages can direct students to any
instructional procedure, they may be written at any
level. For instance, when self-instructional packages
are used in a systems approach, activities such as
seminars may be repeated at regular intervals--or
called for by students. In such circumstances,
learning devices or approaches normally not considered
as part of self-paced instruction may be a viable component of a self-instructional package.

When self-instructional packages are used by students outside of a system, and completely independently, they may include objectives at the higher cognitive
levels. However, the speed of learning will not be as
great as alternative procedures specifically designed
for the accomplishment of the higher order objectives.

INTERACTION TECHNIQUES

Interaction techniques hold considerable promise
as devices that can be consistently adapted for use in
development of higher cognitive skills. Among interaction techniques are the wide range of types of discussions and the use of discussions as a part of other
strategies, such as discovery learning, simulations
and games, panels, and inquiry learning.

Simulations and Games

It is an intriguing quirk of fate that simulations and games, which are viewed by some as a frill or waste of time, actually can provide students with opportunities along the full range of cognitive levels. Coupled with their potential for generating enthusiasm, games and simulations offer a powerful teaching tool. Their greatest drawback is the inability of educators to be creative enough to appropriately structure the learning environments necessary to maximize their potential.

In a social science class, for instance, it is possible to simulate representative governmental agencies and lay groups with a wide range of conflicting interests. In the subsequent interactions, students representing one group or another will need to Understand their roles and operating procedures, Apply those procedures in routine matters, Analyze problems to suggest possible solutions and predict consequences, make Judgments as to the best solutions, and Create new or unique solutions.

Under the direction of a master teacher, such simulations offer the closest approximation of the intellectual skills necessary to solve adult life problems that the classroom is likely to provide.

Discovery Learning

For purposes of this discussion, several of the types of teaching procedures sometimes classed as discovery learning (one of the forms of Information Processing) are treated generally here using concept learning as representative. The general intent of this type of discovery learning is to use a higher-level cognitive skill to teach a concept, principle, or procedure that is then retained at the Understanding level or used at the Applying level. It is the position of the discovery learning advocate that this strategy assists students to retain the knowledge gained better and longer, and to apply any principles Understood with greater facility.

As an example of concept learning in its simplest form, a primary teacher who wishes to teach geometric

shapes would not simply display triangles and define
and explain them. Rather, a series of geometric
shapes would be shown, and students would be asked to
indicate what shapes that followed the first one
(triangle) were similar to it. When the children had
properly indicated the triangles that followed, a
discussion would be initiated in which the similarities
and differences between the shapes would be developed
by students. Proper responses would be reinforced and
improper responses redirected. Ultimately the students
would evolve a working definition of triangles. Thus
the concept of triangles is "discovered" through the
induction of characteristics. When students are
finished, the net result is an Understanding of triangles. The process used to develop the concept was
Analysis. The ultimate information gained, however,
is at the Understanding level.

Panels, Reports, and Debates

Common techniques used by many teachers are those
in which selected students serve as the focus of the
teaching act for brief periods, in place of the teacher. In these instances, a certain amount of interaction takes place. While the potential for higher-
order learning during these periods of interaction
exists, the teacher must often take "pot luck" as to
the actual amount generated.

The teacher who can utilize the cognitive domain
classification model is, however, in a much better
position to encourage higher-level thinking. This is
because he can reinforce certain avenues of student
interaction that involve Analyzing and Judging, and
can redirect those that do not. The problem is, of
course, that the teacher must be judicious in his
interjections so as to promote proper direction during
interaction periods without dominating a very large
percentage of the total interaction time. Without
some teacher interjection, opportunities for higher-
level thought may be lost. With too much teacher
interjection, the effect of the student-directed
structure will be minimized.

INQUIRY LEARNING

In its fundamental form, inquiry learning is
simply an attempt to apply the scientific method to

the classroom, regardless of content area. The theory
is that since problems and questions do emerge during
the course of studying a topic, it is often desirable
to deal with them using an inquiry strategy based on
steps in the scientific method.

Suppose, for instance, that an eighth grade
history class is studying the events leading to World
War II, and has expressed dismay over the amount of
destruction to the U.S. fleet at Pearl Harbor. The
teacher sees an opportunity to use an inquiry strategy.
Below are the steps of the scientific method applied
to this situation, classified at appropriate levels
within the cognitive classification model.

> General Problem--The class reacts to the amount
> of destruction to the U.S. fleet at Pearl
> Harbor on December 7, 1941.

For the class, this realization may also be an
affective domain Reacting level response. But it
should be accompanied by an Understanding of the actual
extent of damage.

> Definition of Problem--The class focuses on
> the specific question as to why the U.S.
> forces were so ill-prepared for the attack.

After discussion, the students' inquiry begins to
focus on a specific problem. It could be one of
several, but the process of attempting to ferret out
what the key question is, or the question that will
reflect the tone of the class, is a matter of Analyzing
the suggested ideas and problem statements, and Judging
which of them will be most satisfactory for the purposes (or intent) of the class.

> Formulating an Hypothesis--The class decides
> on the hypothesis, "The United States' lack
> of preparedness was a result of a series of
> poor judgments by the U.S. government and
> the military."

The same set of intellectual skills as the previous step are used again, culminating in the Creating
of a possible hypothesis. Based on the limited data

available to the class at the time, the teacher directs the interaction to the formulation of various hypotheses, until a consensus is reached as to the most satisfactory suggestion. This "best guess" will be the object of further investigation.

This process focuses on the skills of Analysis, followed by Judging and Creating. As class members submit the facts that they already possess during discussion, the teacher encourages them to put these facts together to Unite Ideas resulting in several hypotheses. Each of these is then Judged on its merits, and the one most likely to be correct is selected.

Structuring a Data-gathering Procedure--The class is organized into several groups, with each one being responsible for collecting specific types of data.

This process is ideally undertaken at the Analysis level. The students group themselves by data-gathering categories. Each group works to induce the characteristics of a conceptual model of the type of data they will gather that will provide useful input. It is also common for the teacher to simply assign students to the groups and explain the characteristics of their data-gathering category. When this procedure is followed, it lowers the cognitive level of the step to Understanding.

Gathering Data--Each group functions independently to seek and record data pertinent to its category.

Students engaged in the operation of data gathering are Applying and Analyzing. They first use whatever rules and principles they Understand (either from prior experience or from specific directions provided by the teacher for this purpose) to locate potentially useful information (Applying). They then classify the data found as being or not being within their category (Analyzing).

It is during the course of this process that students may wish to reformulate their hypothesis. Since the initial hypothesis was based on limited data, and

92

more data are now available to the students, the initial "guess" may be deemed inadequate or incorrect. Also, students are aware that other groups are gathering other data, and all aspects of the problem must be investigated before the hypothesis is accepted or rejected.

Analysis of Data--All of the data are organized into pro, con, and neutral categories, which support, refute, or have no effect on the hypothesis.

As each piece of data is presented by the respective groups, it is classified into one of the three categories: pro, con, or neutral. Although the process is called "Analyzing Data" in the steps of the scientific method, the group may well encounter data that will not clearly fall into one of the three categories. When this happens, the class must exercise a Judgment.

This process is best accomplished in a style that allows an overall view or perspective of the evidence, usually on the chalkboard or overhead projector. After the initial classifications are completed, a set of Judgments may be made in which each piece of data is weighed. The weight of evidence on one side may be more than balanced by the power of a counterpart. These evaluations take place at the Judging level.

Conclusions--The hypothesis is accepted or rejected.

Finally, the ultimate Judgment is made whether to accept or reject the hypothesis. It is also possible, of course, that the data gathered on the pro side may balance with the data on the con side, and no firm conclusion can be reached. This conclusion, or a decision to accept or reject the hypothesis, again reflects higher-level thought. At this point, it is possible for the class to formulate additional hypotheses (that grow out of the initial one) for further investigation.

Thus it becomes apparent that this method of inquiry utilizes a wide array of the cognitive processes as defined by the cognitive classification model, with

considerable emphasis at the highest levels. It is, in
effect, a way to organize and direct discussions for
the purpose of stimulating higher levels of thinking.

DISCUSSIONS

It should be obvious at this point that the discussion format is an integral part of many strategies
for teaching. This is because the discussion format
offers an efficient approach for getting at the higher-
level cognitive processes. The interaction between
people continuously offers the participants opportunities to become involved in higher-order cognitive
thinking.

When a student is involved in a discussion, he
listens to statements made by other students or the
teacher. When considered thoughtfully, the content of
the statements is compared with the experience of the
listener (an Analyzing process). The similarities and
differences between the facts (as perceived by the
listener), and the stated perceptions of others, are
examined. From this comparison a set of rationales
for a Judgment is established and a conclusion is
drawn. This Judgment may be agreement or disagreement.
If it is disagreement, hopefully the student will be
motivated to participate in the discussion, sharing
his reasons for that disagreement.

This process is different from the superficial
type of off-hand statements encountered in "bull-
sessions." Too often in their efforts to engage students in higher-order thinking, teachers allow what
could be opportunities for higher thought to degenerate
into a series of prejudicial opinions (shared igno-
rance). When this happens, it can be because there
was not enough preliminary investigation to give the
students sufficient data to make valid comparisons,
and/or because the teacher does not use probing questions to force students to support their Judgments.

STRATEGIES TO INSPIRE COGNITIVE CREATING

As has been implied previously, the teacher most
often works on the intellectual levels of Understanding, Applying, Analyzing, and Judging. It is the

position of the authors that teachers can and should also make serious attempts to work with students at the Cognitive Creating level. Behavioral objectives can only be written at the 6.1--Uniting Ideas level. That is, the teacher has within his power the ability to structure situations to inspire Creative Insight, but whether such insights will actually take place is a moot question.

It is well to point out that the Creative Insight that is referred to at this level has varying descriptors. Such experiences might be labeled "an inspiration," the "a-ha!" effect, the "light bulb" effect, the "intuitive leap," or the "skipping of intellectual stages." The moment may emerge accompanied by an affective reaction that sweeps over the individual like a flash of lightning, complete with the adrenalin gland "squish," or may so quietly become a part of a solution that there is little realization that it has taken place. In the case of the former, the adjectives posed above are applicable. In the case of the latter, the creative nature of the solution may never be realized.

Additionally, the control a teacher or an individual has over such phenomena is sketchy, and occurrence may take place at any time without attempts to produce it. However, a likely time for such phenomena to occur is when engaged in the Uniting of Ideas, and when arrangements for ideational diverging have been made.

The quantity of teaching arrangements, strategies, and methods available to encourage creative thought is unwieldy. There are too many to review separately, but not enough to effect a good classification which yields convenient subgroups that can be analyzed because of their similarities. Therefore, a list of methods and educational programs for stimulating creativity has been included in Appendix E. This list was assembled by Sidney Parnes.[3]

In place of an analysis of many separate methods, a two-pronged attack is substituted here. First, a general set of guidelines for teachers, applicable in a variety of settings, is described; second, the most common of the teacher strategies, brainstorming, is examined.

TEACHER GUIDELINES TO
STIMULATE CREATIVITY

According to Ralph J. Hallman, "Research literature supports the position that creativity indeed can
be taught, but that it cannot be taught by the traditional authoritarian methods. Creative procedures
cannot be prescribed nor can they be written into
lesson plans; yet creative teaching is the best way,
perhaps the only way, to promote creative behavior on
the part of the pupil."[4] Although the authors would
insist that classroom environments can be structured
to stimulate creativity, Hallman's basic premise, that
creativity may best be produced as a function of
spontaneity, is worth noting. It is well, then, to
note several teacher behaviors which Hallman and others
have identified as those which stand the highest chance
of inspiring creative activity.

1. Provide a rich environment. When the learning
environment has many stimulating artifacts, accessible
to students, the possibility of creative insights
occurring may be enhanced.

2. Avoid rigid rule structures. When students
are allowed to move, explore physically as well as
mentally, without fear of rigidity, creativity is
more likely to occur.

3. Allow students to explore their own areas of
interest. Whenever possible, capitalize upon student-
centered ideas and interests to maintain and increase
motivation.

4. Ask probing questions that encourage students
to relate data, clarify data, and amplify data.

5. Ask divergent questions that encourage students to suggest answers that are unique and imaginative.

6. Encourage students to break down big problems
into small problems, and to take small problems and
make larger problem areas from them.

7. Directly reward imaginative thinking with
positive reinforcement, and point out such instances
to all students.

8. <u>Avoid</u> <u>evaluative</u> <u>judgments</u> by allowing students to render such judgments themselves, thus allowing more variety at building judgmental criteria.

Brainstorming

Brainstorming is most often thought of as a process for gathering a large group of ideas quickly, without an initial concern for the quality of those ideas. Generally, a discussion leader begins by structuring a problem or situation, all members of the group contribute ideas as rapidly as possible, and these ideas are recorded for later analysis and judgment.

Brainstorming is based on the premise that few people have been taught to think creatively, but rather critically, and that not all problems are best solved by critical thinking. It simply attempts to tap into the "unconscious" or "insight" possibilities by lowering external blocks commonly inhibiting groups or individuals.

There are many unanswered questions regarding brainstorming as a method for realizing the Creative Insight level, but some generalizations may be possible:

1. Attitudes of group members toward each other do not seem to improve because of solutions in problem-solving situations using traditional methods.[5]

2. The quality of solutions in problem-solving situations using brainstorming seems to be higher than the quality of solutions using traditional methods.[6]

3. In some brainstorming circumstances, women are able to outperform men.[7]

4. After brainstorming, deferring judgments about solutions seems to lead to better-quality solutions.[8]

In the brainstorming technique, the order of events does not follow a sequentially rising order through the intellectual levels. At the initial stages, the teacher is attempting to first gain an Understanding of the process, possibly Analyzing the problem at hand, and then moving to an environmental structure than can allow ideational diverging that hopefully will draw out some Creatively Insightful ideas. These ideas are then cycled back through Analysis, culminating in Cognitive Judgments.

CONCLUSION

The cognitive classification model provides a fresh perspective for viewing any of the many teaching procedures commonly utilized in the classroom. If teachers clearly possess the ability to determine at what cognitive levels their teaching strategies function, they can ensure variety and consistency, and thereby enhance the quantity and quality of learning.

ENDNOTES

[1]During this chapter, words referring to levels within the cognitive classification model are capitalized. This is done in an effort to remind the reader that these words have specific meanings as defined in Chapter Two.

[2]See Walter D. Pierce and Howard G. Getz, "Relationships Among Teaching, Cognitive Levels, Testing and IQ," Illinois School Research, 6 (Winter 1973):27-31.

[3]Sidney J. Parnes, "Methods and Educational Programs for Stimulating Creativity: A Representative List," Creative Behavior Guidebook (New York: Charles Scribner's Sons, 1967), pp. 300-02.

[4]Ralph J. Hallman, "Techniques of Creative Teaching," The Journal of Creative Behavior, 1 (July 1967): 327.

[5]H. Ariei, "Brainstorming is a Way of Facilitating Creative Thinking," Dissertation Abstracts, 25:6311-12, 1965.

[6] Ibid.

[7] H. C. Lindgren and F. Lindgren, "Brainstorming and Orneriness as Facilitators of Creativity," _Psychological Reports_, 16 (1965):577-83; and H. C. Lindgren and F. Lindgren, "Creativity, Brainstorming and Orneriness: A Cross-Cultural Study," _Journal of Social Psychology_, 16 (1965):23-30.

[8] A. Meadow, S. J. Parnes, and H. Reese, "Influence of Brainstorming Instructions and Problem Sequence on a Creative Problem-Solving Test," _Journal of Applied Psychology_, 43 (1959):413-16; and S. J. Parnes and A. Meadows, "Effects of Brainstorming Instructions on Creative Problem Solving by Trained and Untrained Subjects," _Journal of Educational Psychology_, 50 (1959): 171-76.

CHAPTER VI--<u>Strategies</u> <u>in</u> <u>the</u> <u>Use</u>
<u>of</u> <u>the</u> <u>Affective</u> Domain

DEFINING AFFECTIVE BEHAVIOR,
GOALS, AND TEACHER ROLE

AFFECTS

The affective domain classification model
introduced in Chapter Three presented affective behavior in a "developmental sequence," using as a sorting
factor an increasing degree of cognition for each
progressive level. As a whole, the six affective
categories provide a definition of affective behavior.
At this point, however, it is helpful to define the
term "affect" in a more conventional way (i.e., by
means of a classificatory or generic definition).
Such a definition specifies those characteristics (or
attributes) that differentiate affects from other
forms of behavior. Since each affective level is dis-
tinguished from any other level by the degree of cognition, clarifying the conceptual meaning of affective
behavior can simplify the task of selecting and/or
developing teaching strategies appropriate for affective education.

For purposes of analysis, "affects" are
viewed as a three-part process wherein a specific
<u>environmental</u> <u>stimulus</u> triggers an <u>internal</u> response,
culminating in an <u>observable</u> <u>behavior</u> on the part of
the individual. This three-part breakdown provides a
useful way of conceptualizing the total process, even
though only the stimulus and behavior are observable.

101

Thus, an operational definition of an "affect" can be formulated as follows: "An _affect_ is any type, or degree, of positive or negative feeling toward environmental circumstances, expressed by means of an observable display of emotive, reactive, or evaluative behavior." Such a definition depicts in general terms what apparently occurs at any given level or sublevel of the affective domain classification system. Since the level (or quality) of an affect is a function of the "degree of cognition," estimates of affective levels can be derived from observations of student behaviors in given circumstances.

ATTITUDES AND VALUES

Two other concepts are frequently used in discussions of the affective domain--_attitudes_ and _values_. It is helpful to understand the meaning of these two concepts and to indicate how they are related to the concept "affect" and to the affective domain classification model. Attitudes are usually associated with the feelings, preferences, or aversions individuals may have toward certain things. They are those feelings and inclinations which the individual has not thought through or reflected on in depth. Hence, attitudes can be thought of as largely unexamined inclinations or dispositions for or against particular objects, ideas, or actions. They serve as general "feeling indicators" that usually influence behavior. On the other hand, when someone _values_ something he assigns worth to it with reference to personal goals and purposes. This, then, implies an examination of the valued object in terms of the individual's life and experience. Thus, values amount to tested dispositional insights for or against particular objects, ideas, or actions. They serve as specific guides for consistent behavior.

Therefore, when an individual is confronted with an object or idea which he _values_ or has an _attitude_ toward, he is likely to engage in affective behavior. Attitudes, as defined above, are most closely related to affective behaviors at the Reacting and Conforming levels, whereas values imply behaviors at the higher levels. When students are operating at the Reacting and Conforming levels, they reflect an _attitudinal_ stance; when they are operating at the Validating level and above, they are involved in developing,

102

examining, and relating <u>values</u>.

GENERAL AFFECTIVE GOALS

In certain respects, the focus of affective education is essentially the same for all subject areas. It is common to hear teachers talk about how important it is for students to behave properly in the classroom, and to acquire good work habits and high ideals (or ethical standards). In the context of the teaching-learning environment, these areas of concern are intimately related to the affective domain. They can be conceptualized as general affective goals of three types: (1) behavioral attitudes and values (such as concern with how one should behave as a student); (2) procedural attitudes and values (such as concern with how one should proceed as an inquirer and learner); and (3) substantive attitudes and values (such as concern with how one should live and view life).[1]

<u>Behavioral Goals</u> are attitudes and values that are related to the classroom procedures that are necessary if the teaching-learning process is to proceed. The concern is mainly with demonstrating respect for the rights, feelings, and property of others (including the teacher and the school).

<u>Procedural Goals</u> are attitudes and values that are related to the mode of rational inquiry that is necessary if ideas and propositions are to be analyzed and tested. The concern is mainly with demonstrating respect for critical thinking, objectivity, evidence, and logical analysis.

<u>Substantive Goals</u> are attitudes and values that are related to the nature of the "good life" and how it might be achieved. The concern is with economic, social, political, ethical, and aesthetic questions and issues of importance to a pluralistic society.

Many educators maintain that since certain behavioral and procedural attitudes and values are essential to the educational enterprise they should be <u>taught directly</u> in the school, whereas substantive attitudes

and values should be taught about and examined by means
of value clarification and value analysis procedures.
However, other educators suggest that behavioral and
procedural attitudes and values also should be examined,
clarified, and analyzed in the pedagogical setting. A
further issue is the problem of deciding which levels
of the affective domain classification system students
should be expected to attain with respect to particular
behavioral, procedural, and substantive goals. For
example, should the teacher be satisfied with a given
procedural attitude at the Conforming level, or should
he expect students to be able to deal with such
affects at the Validating level and above? When dealing with particular substantive values, is Validating
sufficient, or should the teacher encourage students
to deal with the value at the Affective Judging level?

The resolution of important questions such as
those posed above require the teacher to make professional decisions firmly based upon a rational philosophical view of the goals and purposes of education.
Although it is beyond the scope of this book to provide guidelines for the development of a philosophy of
education, the discussions of the affective domain included here are intended to emphasize the need for a
defensible philosophical stance on the part of the
teacher. The discussions of teaching strategies in
subsequent sections of this chapter should be particularly helpful to the teacher who is in the process of
examining his position(s) relative to affective education.

RATIONALE FOR TEACHER ROLE

Teachers are often concerned about what their role
should be when value issues are brought up and/or
examined in the classroom. Should the teacher,
(1) try to avoid controversy?; (2) try to be the impar-
tial (and neutral) arbitrator?; or (3) attempt to
instill in students acceptable values? Two social
studies educators advocate the role of "defensible
partisanship" as appropriate for teachers in a cul-
turally pluralistic and democratically oriented society. They state their position in the following manner.

We accept the concept of "defensible partisanship" as an appropriate position for the teacher to assume in dealing with value-laden propositions. Defensible partisanship assumes that the teacher inevitably makes preferential choices among competing ethical alternatives and creates the conditions in the classroom for choices based on the most rational criteria. The teacher takes the position that methods of value analysis and discussion which are consistent with our democratic ideals produce the most defensible conclusions. Thus the teacher is partisan for selecting the method of inquiry as the most appropriate means to adjudicate values and for taking a stand and helping others to take a stand on a social issue based on this process of inquiry. As a matter of strategy, the teacher should be very careful to avoid introduction of his judgments prematurely. He should give the students the opportunity to make their beliefs explicit and then reflect upon them. At crucial points the teacher may want to present his own considered thoughts on the subject if he sees that the perspective of the learners will be broadened by them. In no way should the teacher assume the role of the authority in determining good and evil, ugly and beautiful, moral and immoral. His position is that of a fellow inquirer, one who constantly seeks the truth and the ethically defensible. His basic attitude is that values are not taught but that they are critically examined.[2]

RELATIONSHIP BETWEEN OBJECTIVES, LEARNING ACTIVITIES, AND EVALUATIONS

The vagueness traditionally associated with the affective domain has led to considerable confusion on the part of both curriculum developers and practicing teachers. The result has been much "lip service" to the idea of affective education, but very little attention to the development of appropriate instructional programs. Most programs, courses, or units of study with an affective orientation fail to clearly identify and relate affective objectives, learning activities, and evaluative procedures.

It is common practice for teachers and curriculum committees to list many general affective objectives in course descriptions and curriculum guides. However, many such lists turn out to be nothing more than "window dressing" for supervisors, the PTA, or the board of education. All too often the general objectives are not operationalized in terms of specific affective behaviors, related learning activities are not provided, and little attempt is made to assess pupil achievement of the objectives.

Sometimes a teacher who is interested in the affective domain will involve students in a variety of activities with strong affective overtones. The teacher may enjoy the activities and find that students are easily motivated and become enthusiastic when engaged in such pursuits. However, if the affective activities have no specific relationship to course or unit objectives and are not followed up by some type of assessment, they become ends in themselves--merely "busy work," or a form of recess from the cognitive domain. They may be "fun" for all of the participants, but they are not integrated components of a goal-oriented instructional program.

Much confusion and wasted effort in affective education can be traced directly to the commonly held assumption that if students learn about something they will automatically assume a particular stance or attitude toward it (e.g., learning about the facts of a nation's history will produce loyal, patriotic citizens). Understanding content is certainly a necessary condition for forming an opinion or attitude about it, but it does not follow that such knowledge is a sufficient condition for producing a given affective disposition. Frequently a teaching unit will have both cognitive and affective objectives, but only cognitive learning activities and evaluations will be provided. Nevertheless, many teachers using the unit will maintain that the affective objectives were attained as a by-product of cognitive achievement. They know (or feel) this to be the case in spite of the fact that the affective objectives received little or no attention whatsoever in the instructional process. Although there are a number of relationships and parallels between the cognitive and affective domains, it cannot be assumed that learning in the cognitive domain will automatically produce particular outcomes in the affective domain.

As indicated in Chapter Three, the traditional approach to affective education consisted mainly of the selection of socially approved attitudes and values by the teacher (or by the school or community), followed by an attempt to instill students with the values by means of exhortation and/or example. For the most part, as long as students appeared to speak and behave in a manner consistent with the approved values, the teacher--or school--assumed that instruction had been successful. Thus, those students who could be influenced to react in the approved fashion were considered properly socialized into the culture. Such an approach to affective education is concerned primarily with the Reacting and Conforming levels of the affective domain, with limited opportunities for students to deal with their ideas and feelings at the higher affective levels.

An interesting by-product of the traditional approach is that those students who raise questions about or object to what is being "instilled" may achieve higher level affective outcomes than is the case for those who quickly conform. This comes about due to the fact that the "objectors" are often exposed to a reasoned defense of the ideas (and values) and their relationship to the ongoing society (e.g., they may be exposed to Validating, Affective Judging, and so forth). Of course, many students who "object" are merely suppressed or punished for their "poor" attitudes; hence, their affective education becomes something quite different from what was intended. It is the position of this book that students should have opportunities to move beyond the Conforming level with respect to the wide range of ideas, behaviors, and other input encountered in school. The movement to higher affective levels should not be limited to chance happenings for a few brave souls who question what is essentially a process of indoctrination.

As is the case for the other two domains, pre-assessment procedures are extremely important for instruction in the affective realm. Even for well-planned units of instruction with comprehensive evaluations, the teacher will be unable to draw valid conclusions about what has been accomplished if

107

pre-assessment data are lacking. The student attitudes
and values in evidence at the conclusion of instruction
may or may not be the same as those held prior to
instruction. Without appropriate pre-assessment the
teacher has no evidence of affective growth.

Affective objectives should be stated as specifically as possible in terms of desired levels of the
affective classification model. In most instances,
the intent of such objectives is to promote behavior
at a level higher than the one at which students are
operating, although on occasion the intent might be
merely to encourage continued replications of behavior
at a particular level. As students move to higher
levels the degree of cognition increases, and this
implies added attention to the task of examining, re-
fining, and relating affective behaviors. Whatever
the intent of the objectives, sound educational practice requires that relevant learning activities be
provided and that evaluative procedures be employed
that are designed to determine the degree to which the
objectives have been achieved. However, if the objectives, learning activities, and evaluations are not
developed with reference to previously collected pre-
assessment data, the results of the instructional
enterprise amount to nothing more than guesswork.

USING THE AFFECTIVE CLASSIFICATION MODEL
IN PLANNING

The affective domain classification model provides
a conceptual framework designed to serve as a frame-of-
reference and a guide for instructional planning in the
affective domain. In particular, the model can be of
assistance to the teacher in the preparation of affective objectives that are clear, precise, and logically
related to the developmental sequence of affective
behavior.

Prior to the formulation of affective objectives
for a given unit of instruction, it is important for
the teacher to assess the subject-matter background
and related affective orientations of his students.
Estimates of affective levels can be derived from systematic observations of students in various activities,
situations, and tasks related to the subject area. On
the basis of the pre-assessment data, the teacher can

deduce which affective level (or levels) is in need of
attention. Thereupon the teacher can proceed to develop objectives that clearly describe the desired level(s)
of affective behavior.

What follows are guidelines designed to help the
teacher determine the kinds of affective behaviors to
include in objectives at each level. They are intended
to provide a general overview of what can be accomplished at each level.

GUIDELINES FOR AFFECTIVE
PERCEIVING OBJECTIVES

When operating primarily at the Affective Perceiving level, the student is responding internally to
experience. The actual extent and quality of such perception is determined by the external responses at the
Reacting level. Hence, in practice, conventional
instructional objectives would not be developed
specifically for this level. However, since Affective
Perceiving is a product of encounters with the environment (experience) and the assignment of meaning to such
experiences, the teacher can employ experiential objectives and a variety of lower-level cognitive objectives
as a means of stimulating--or triggering--Affective
Perceiving. The following guidelines should assist the
teacher in developing appropriate objectives related to
this level:

1. Develop cognitive objectives related to par-
    ticular segments of content likely to have
    affective overtones for students.

2. Develop experiential objectives designed to
    promote student involvement with the desired
    content.

GUIDELINES FOR
REACTING OBJECTIVES

When operating primarily at the lower Reacting
level the student displays emotion and, on occasion,
may be able to demonstrate slight or partial awareness
of the behavior. When operating primarily at the
higher Reacting level the student displays emotion and
can be expected to discuss the behavior (and feelings)

and the stimulus that prompted them. The following
are intended as general guidelines to assist the teacher in developing objectives at this level:

After a display of undifferentiated, involuntary,
or habitual emotional behavior, the student will
make a notation of the occurrence of the behavior
(including whatever descriptive data he can remember).

When confronted with a particular concept, object,
or idea, the student will describe his behavior
and feelings toward the concept.

When confronted with a particular concept, object,
or idea, the student will discuss the nature of
his past and present reactions to the concept, and
whether or not he should continue to react in the
same way.

GUIDELINES FOR
CONFORMING OBJECTIVES

When operating primarily at the Conforming level,
the student can be expected to select a convenient
rationale or reason in support of his behavior and
feelings toward something. The following is intended
as a general guideline to assist the teacher in developing objectives at this level:

When confronted with a particular concept, object,
or idea, and after describing his behavior and
feelings toward it, the student will supply an
expedient or conventional rationale or reason in
support of the behavior and feelings.

GUIDELINES FOR
VALIDATING OBJECTIVES

When operating primarily at the Validating level,
the student can be expected to examine objectively the
rationale or reasons offered in support of particular
behavior and feelings toward something, followed by
acceptance, rejection, or revision of the initial
rationale, behavior, and feelings. The following is
intended as a guideline to assist the teacher in
developing objectives at this level:

When confronted with a particular concept, object, or idea, the student (1) will become involved in an objective investigation of the validity of the rationale or reason used in support of his behavior and feelings toward the concept; and (2) will accept, reject, or revise the original stance or position on the basis of the findings of the investigation.

GUIDELINES FOR AFFECTIVE JUDGING OBJECTIVES

When operating primarily at the Affective Judging level, the student can be expected to relate accepted (and validated) value positions to his total value system and develop criteria for ordering and choosing between accepted value positions. Also, at this level the student can be expected to choose between accepted value positions in conflicting situations on the basis of specific value criteria. The following are intended as guidelines to assist the teacher in developing objectives at this level:

When confronted with two or more concepts, objects, or ideas about which he has validated value positions, the student will develop and/or articulate specific criteria that provide the basis for ordering and choosing between the value positions.

When confronted with a situation where two or more validated value positions are in conflict, the student (1) will choose one of the value positions as a means of resolving the dilemma; and (2) will clearly specify the value criteria that served as the basis for the choice.

GUIDELINES FOR AFFECTIVE CREATING OBJECTIVES

When operating primarily at the Affective Creating level, the student can be expected to utilize the creative imagination to produce value configurations that are unusual, unique, and insightful. Unfortunately, little is known about the workings of the creative imagination or exactly how it is activated. It may well be that achievement of a variety of higher order cognitive and affective objectives stimulate creative thinking. Many scholars in the field of creativity maintain that the "climate"(or environment) is the crucial variable; the necessary (but not sufficient) condition for creativity.

At the lower Affective Creating level, (i.e., Integrating Values), the student examines, probes, and explores major segments of his value system and produces a reorganized and more fully integrated value system. The following is intended as a general guideline to assist the teacher in developing objectives that may promote integration:

When confronted with one or more concepts, objects, or ideas about which he has validated value positions, the student will relate and classify the value positions with other values (and with related value judgments and value criteria) in terms of similarity, consistency, compatibility, and practical applications.

At the higher Affective Creating level (i.e., Inspirational Insight), the student focuses thought on ways of changing, altering, and reformulating major segments of his value system and produces unique insights about new values and new value configurations. One approach that can be used in developing objectives for this level is to emphasize the conditions (i.e., "climate") under which the student will operate, and then to specify that under these conditions the student will be encouraged to create a unique idea (or product). What follows is a general guideline that may be of assistance to the teacher interested in creating an environment wherein inspirational insights may occur:

Given a particular value issue or problem that is of concern to the student, and an environment (climate) that is supportive, nonthreatening, rewarding, and ideationally diverse, the student will attempt to develop a completely new way of viewing and/or dealing with the value issue.

The affective classification model can be used as an aid in developing sets of objectives for any particular topic or content area. The sources for affective objectives are as diverse as life itself, since affective behavior pervades all aspects of human experience. Hence, in practice, the affective domain cannot be isolated from the other two domains. Affective objectives can be generated which are closely related to the affective overtones of many life experiences, or they can be the affective counterparts of particular cognitive or psychomotor objectives.

The development of affective objectives begins with the selection of a particular topic, idea, experience, or skill as the focus for affective behavior. The next step is to identify the specific levels of affective behavior that are sought in the instructional setting. The final task is the actual writing of objectives appropriate for each level. For example, the topic of <u>poetry</u> <u>as</u> <u>a</u> <u>form</u> <u>of</u> <u>expression</u> might be selected for a high school English class and the teacher wants to generate objectives for all six affective levels. The following objectives illustrate what might be done.

<u>Affective</u>
<u>Perceiving</u>:   The student will become involved in a <u>classroom</u> <u>experience</u> wherein a group of talented speech and drama students will present an idea (of importance to the class) in four different forms, namely: (1) in formal prose, (2) in "street language," (3) in a brief dramatic presentation, and (4) in a poetic form. The presentations will be followed by an open-ended, give-and-take discussion between the actors and the class, focusing upon the meaning and/or impact of the idea in each form.

<u>Reacting</u>:   While listening to the recitation of two poems, the student will draw or write anything he wishes on a blank sheet of paper as an expression of his emotional response.

Immediately after hearing a professional actor read a series of short poems, the student will briefly express his personal reaction and feelings about poetry in writing, speech, and/or action.

113

Conforming: After a general class discussion about poetry as a form of expression, the student will specify in writing his reasons for acting and feeling as he does when confronted with poetry.

Validating: After hearing the teacher read several poems, and reading twelve selected poems, the student will re-examine his current attitude toward poetry, and will prepare a two-page paper explaining why he intends to maintain, revise, or discard his present stance or position on poetry.

Affective Judging: After a class discussion of several forms of expression, the student will list in order of preference five important contemporary modes of expression (including poetry), and then will describe, in a paragraph, the criteria he employed in deciding how to rank the various modes.

Given a choice between reading poetry or engaging in two other activities of approximately equal value (or dis-value) to the student, the student will choose one activity, and when asked will clearly specify the reasoning used in making the decision.

Affective Creating: The student will prepare an oral report that attempts to show the degree of consistency between his accepted value position about poetry and his value positions concerning three other forms of expression (such as science fiction, TV dramas, rock music, modern art, and so on).

In a supportive, nonthreatening environment, the student will be asked to express the fundamental elements of his philosophy of life

in a poem of not more than thirty
words, and share the completed poem
with other members of the class.
Consequentially, the student will
be asked to repeat the above task
two or three times, but each new
version of the poem must be only
one-half the length of the previous
version. Finally, the student will
be asked to prepare a final draft
of his philosophical stance in a
poem of whatever length (and with
whatever content adjustment) is
deemed appropriate and desirable.

The same pattern can be followed in generating objectives for other content areas. The behavioral,
procedural, and substantive affective goals of each
subject area can serve as the basis for the development
of specific objectives. Often, a given substantive
goal will be of primary concern to only one content
area, whereas many procedural and behavioral goals will
be of importance to several subject areas. The following list of topics could be used to generate a variety
of affective objectives in the social studies area;
however, the topics related to procedural and behavioral goals would be appropriate for many other areas.

Substantive Area:

1. Capital punishment;
2. Dropping A-bomb on Hiroshima;
3. Assassination of Julius Caesar;
4. Abortion;
5. Détente with China and Russia;
6. Watergate scandals;
7. Busing and racial integration;
8. Women's rights;
9. Gun control;
10. Policies involved in acquisition of
    Panama Canal;
11. Arms control;
12. Capitalism;
13. Lincoln's decision to issue Emancipation
    Proclamation;
14. Socialism.

<u>Procedural</u> <u>Area</u>:

1. Use of reason in dealing with ideas and issues;
2. Use of evidence as a test for accuracy;
3. Objectivity in examining all sides of ideas and issues;
4. Skepticism (or a questioning stance) toward ideas and issues.

<u>Behavioral</u> <u>Area</u>:

1. Student behaviors toward other students. Examples:

   - Permitting others to have their turn in a discussion;

   - Insulting others because of their ideas.

2. Student behaviors toward the teacher. Examples:

   - Failing to pay attention to directions;

   - Respecting teacher's role as moderator.

3. Student behaviors toward school equipment and materials. Examples:

   - Returning borrowed equipment in good condition;

   - Tearing pages out of library book.

Once affective objectives have been formulated, the next step in planning is the selection (or development) of appropriate teaching strategies. In the context of effective instructional planning, teaching strategies are viewed as the <u>instructional</u> <u>means</u> for achieving affective objectives; they must be preceded by proper diagnosis and followed by careful assessment. In the remaining sections of this chapter, a number of teaching strategies are described which are appropriate for achieving various types of affective objectives.

CLASSIFICATION OF AFFECTIVE
TEACHING STRATEGIES

TYPES OF AFFECTIVE
TEACHING STRATEGIES

In contemporary educational literature the rubrics affective education and values education are
used interchangeably. No useful purpose would be
served in attempting to make a special distinction between the two terms; hence, they will be used synony-
mously in the following discussion of teaching
strategies. Three reasonably distinct types of
teaching strategies have emerged from recent values
(or affective) education literature. The three approaches are: (1) value clarification, (2) value
analysis, and (3) moral reasoning.

VALUE CLARIFICATION

Value clarification refers to a variety of teaching strategies that are designed primarily to make
students aware of the attitudes and values that they
(and others) tend to hold or accept. On occasion,
such strategies encourage students to discover and
examine the manner or means by which particular values
came to be "accepted." Value clarification may focus
upon the student's own values, the values of peers and
adults, important societal values, or the values of
other cultures. Although clarification strategies may
encourage students to re-examine attitudes and values,
they do not provide specific procedures for testing
the validity of value positions in a rigorous fashion.
Thus, for the most part, value clarification is diagnostic, descriptive, and open-ended, and little attention is given to helping the student learn how to
develop, test, or judge value positions.

VALUE ANALYSIS

Value analysis refers to teaching strategies that
are specifically designed to involve students in learning a process that will be helpful to them in developing clear, consistent, and empirically valid systems of
belief. Strategies of this type are often referred to

as value inquiry, since they proceed in a manner similar to the scientific method. Value analysis strategies include: (1) "clarification" of value positions, (2) determination of warrants for value positions, (3) testing of warrants, and (4) the application of particular value positions in a variety of situations and circumstances. The emphasis is upon empirical analysis, testing, and practical application.

MORAL REASONING

Moral reasoning refers to the mode of thinking (or orientation) that comes into play when an individual encounters a situation where a choice must be made between accepted values (i.e., a value conflict or dilemma). Teaching strategies designed to promote moral reasoning confront students with value conflicts (or dilemmas) that can be resolved only by making a choice between accepted values. After making the value choices, students are asked to describe the mode of reasoning employed. Moral reasoning strategies provide students with (1) experience in resolving value conflicts, (2) opportunities to observe the reasoning of others, and (3) the option of adopting broader and more flexible modes of reasoning (e.g., higher developmental stage reasoning, based upon Kohlberg's theory of moral reasoning--see Appendix D).

DESCRIPTIONS OF AFFECTIVE
TEACHING STRATEGIES

VALUE CLARIFICATION STRATEGIES

The basic intent of many clarifying strategies is to prompt the student to display a feeling, emotion, or value position following an encounter or experience of some kind. The teacher may create the total environment in which the encounter occurs, or he may merely allude to a previous experience common to the students. Once the encounter takes place (or is recalled), the teacher poses probing questions designed to stimulate affective responses. The responses may reflect a basic emotion, a reaction, or a value disposition; and sometimes they will be followed by a rationale response. The following diagram depicts the elements involved in such strategies.

118

```
Student          Teacher          Student Affective
Encounter   ───→ Probing   ───→   Response(s):
                                  1.  Basic response
                                  2.  Rationale response(?)
```

The student encounter may consist of a particular event or activity in which the student has been involved, or it may be a teacher-contrived situation such as a single provocative statement, two or more differing ideas, a reading selection, a picture, an artifact, or a film. The probing questions, as well as the student responses, may be oral, written, or even nonverbal in form. Although in most cases questions follow encounters, it is sometimes helpful to pose--or suggest--certain questions during or even before the encounter. In all instances, probing questions should be perceived as nonthreatening by the students involved. Such strategies stimulate Affective Perceiving, and elicit Reacting and sometimes Conforming responses (or behavior).

Other clarifying strategies go a step beyond stimulating and eliciting basic responses and attempt to involve students in examining and thinking about: (1) the nature of the ideas and experiences (i.e., the "encounters"), (2) the nature of the responses made, and (3) the possible reasons for the responses. Such strategies stimulate Reacting and Conforming responses and often encourage the initial phases of Validating behavior.

Clarifying strategies are usually designed to focus student thinking from three particular frames-of-reference. First, thinking can be from the reference point of the individual looking at himself (i.e., his ideas and experiences, responses, and reasons). Second, thinking can be from the reference point of the individual looking at other cultures, groups, and subgroups, past and present; (i.e., their ideas and experiences, responses, and reasons). Third, thinking can be from the reference point of an individual trying both to understand and feel how other individuals feel (or felt) in particular circumstances; (i.e., basically, empathetic understanding). In general, clarifying thinking implies attention to questions such as the following:

119

Personal Frame-of-reference

1. What is X?
2. How do I feel about X?
3. Why do I feel this way about X?

Other Culture/Group Frame-of-reference

1. What is Y?
2. How do they feel about Y?
3. Why do they feel this way about Y?

Individual Empathetic Frame-of-reference

1. What is Z?
2. How does he feel about Z?
3. Why does he feel this way about Z?
4. How would I feel about Z if I were in his place?

Clarifying strategies diagnose, assess, and often lay the necessary groundwork for subsequent value analysis and moral reasoning strategies. Clarifying strategies should not be considered ends in themselves; from both the logical and the psychological standpoint they are incomplete. A variety of clarifying strategies are described in the following paragraphs.

Value Sheet Approach

Raths and his associates have developed what they term the value sheet as a means of eliciting value-related responses from students.[3] The approach consists of confronting students with provocative statements, stories, or sets of questions which have value implications for them. Students complete the value sheets on their own (i.e., read the statement, story, and questions, and write out responses). Later the various student ideas can be shared with the teacher, with the entire class, or used as the basis for discussions in small groups. Two value sheet exercises are presented below.

Value Sheet on Human Worth

Opener: The human being is made up of oxygen, nitrogen, phosphorus, hydrogen, carbon, and calcium. There are also 12½ gallons of water, enough iron to make a small nail, about a saltshaker full of salt, and enough sugar to make one small cube. If one were to put all of this together and try to sell it, the whole thing would be worth about one dollar.

Questions:
1. What is the point of this statement?
2. Are you serious in believing that you are worth more than $1.00? Explain.
3. What are some ways we measure the worth of human beings?
4. Can you list some things you have done which show what you think human beings are worth?

Value Sheet on Speaking Up

Opener: In Germany they came first for the Communists, and I didn't speak up because I wasn't a Communist. Then they came for the Jews, and I didn't speak up because I wasn't a Jew. Then they came for the trade unionists, and I didn't speak up because I wasn't a trade unionist. They they came for the Catholics, and I didn't speak up because I was a Protestant. Then they came for me--and by that time no one was left to speak up. (Pastor Martin Niemoller)

Questions:
1. In a few words, what is the central meaning of this statement?
2. What is the Pastor for and what is he against?
3. Which category are you in? When would they have come for you?

4. What are some things going on in
   our world right now about which
   you might need to speak up?
   List them here:

5. If you are not to speak up, who
   should do it?[4]

In both instances above, the student is confronted
by ideas and circumstances with affective implications.
The suggested questions are designed to promote understanding of the ideas and issues involved, to prompt
individual responses, and to encourage students to
ponder their initial positions and consider the
implications of their reactions in a broader context.
Initially, the strategy is likely to elicit Reacting
responses, but subsequent questions tend to guide students toward the Conforming level, and may possibly
help them to see the need for thinking at the Validating
level.

Value Priority Approach

Another approach for stimulating student value-
responses encourages students to identify a number of
things that are important to them; subsequently, they
are asked to choose between certain of the items
selected. The things identified might be abstract
ideas or rules, ways of behaving, or valued material
objects. In any event, after selecting the valued
items the students are asked to indicate which ones
they can do without "in a pinch" and which ones they
feel they cannot do without. In essence, they are
being asked to make choices between things that they
consider good (or important), thus revealing priorities. The following is an example of this approach.

The Baker's Dozen

The teacher asks each student to list thirteen,
a baker's dozen, of his favorite items around
the house which use PLUGS, that is, which require electricity.

When the students have made their lists, the
teacher says, "Now, please draw a line
through the three which you really could do
without if there were suddenly to be a

122

serious power shortage. It's not that you don't like them, but that you could, if you had to, live without them. O.K., now circle the three which really mean the most to you and which you would hold onto until the very end."5

In using the strategy, it is important for the teacher to make it clear that there is no correct answer as to what one should draw lines through or circle. The exercise should be followed by an open-ended class discussion in which students reveal their choices and exchange ideas about why they made them.

The innovative teacher may develop a number of variations to this basic approach, as long as the student is confronted with a situation where he must first identify several valued things, and then must make choices between some of them. The basic "encounter" in this strategy is that of choosing between goods, and it is likely to be accompanied by a degree of frustration on the part of students. The student is being asked to choose things for which he has the strongest feeling or emotion, and to reject those about which he has weaker feelings. At the outset the strategy involves students at the Reacting and Conforming levels; however, the "choice problem" amounts to a mild value conflict where they will see the need for developing a rationale for choosing. Thus, students are reflecting both values and priorities.

Value Inference Approach

Many students are uncertain what their values are, or even if they have any values. An important role for the teacher interested in value education is to help students identify those ideas, objects, and behaviors that they consider important. One approach for value identification is to ask students to recall a particular act or behavior, speculate about why it occurred as it did, and make inferences about the values of the participants. Subsequently, they can be asked to speculate about their own behavior in the same (or similar) situation and make inferences about their own values. This approach may be summarized in the following way.

123

Identifying Values

After students engage in an activity (i.e., read a story, view a film, role-play), the teacher asks them questions such as the following:

Questions	Student Responses
1. What did the (key figures) do in the story?	-Describes behavior
2. What do you think were their reasons for doing what they did?	-States inferences regarding reasons
3. What do these reasons you've identified tell you about what is important to them?	-States inferences regarding values
4. If you did such and such (teacher specifies a similar situation), what would you do? Why?	-States behavior and gives explanation
5. What does this show about what you think is important?	-States inferences about his own values
6. What differences do you see in what all these people think is important? Similarities?	-Makes comparisons[6]

The basic assumption underlying this approach is that in making inferences about what they and others consider important, students will gain insights into their own values. As they speculate about the reasons--or rationales--for particular actions and behaviors, they are operating mainly at the Conforming level. However, the process is likely to result in unexpected discoveries and insights (about themselves and others), which should encourage them to examine their positions more carefully (thus advancing them to the Validating level).

Authentic Problems Approach

Sometimes the teacher using inquiry teaching may want to stimulate student responses that reflect <u>doubt</u> and <u>concern</u> about their beliefs. A form of psychological arousal often manifests itself when students come to sense inadequacies or inconsistencies in their beliefs, concepts, or values. The arousal is indicative of an authentic problem for the students.

Doubt and concern can be aroused when the teacher creates situations which cast doubt on important beliefs held by all or most of his students. Many ideas and issues can become authentic problems when students are prompted to reflect upon what they believe to be so and find inconsistencies among their beliefs, or when students are prompted to reflect upon new data and find it to be in conflict with what they believe to be so. There are at least two ways in which the teacher can bring such problems into focus in a pedagogical setting:

1. When the teacher makes it clear that one important student belief is in conflict with another important student belief (i.e., a Belief vs. Belief Problem), or

2. When the teacher makes available data which are relevant to and in conflict with a belief held by a substantial number of students (i.e., a Data vs. Belief Problem).[7]

In either instance, an authentic problem has been made apparent. The two variations might be summarized in the manner shown in Figure 4.

Sample <u>Belief</u> <u>vs.</u> <u>Belief</u> Problems

Example #1

Student Belief: Honesty is always the best policy

Student Belief: One should remain loyal to his good friends

125

Authentic Problem	Student Belief(s)	Teacher Creates Problem	Student Response(s)
Belief vs. Belief Problem: Where the consistency of a portion of student system of beliefs is brought into question	Students believe two particular things are so (or right)	Teacher creates a situation wherein it is evident that in certain respects the beliefs are in conflict with each other	Concern and doubt responses (resulting from a degree of cognitive dissonance)
Data vs. Belief Problem: Where the student grounding of a belief is brought into question	Students believe something is so (or right)	Teacher makes available some data that tend to bring the belief into question	Concern and doubt responses (resulting from a degree of cognitive dissonance)

Variations of Approach to an Authentic Problem

Figure 4

Statement
(from teacher):   What would you do if you saw your
                  friend stealing valuable merchan-
                  dise from a jewelry store?

Result: Arousal of doubt and concern
                  responses

Example #2

Student Belief: Everyone should try to be suc-
                  cessful

Student Belief: The kind of a person you are is
                  more important than how success-
                  ful you are

Statement
(from teacher):   Would you rather be a successful
                  business or professional person
                  who is detested by everyone and
                  considered a scoundrel; or a very
                  poor person who everyone consid-
                  ers to be a wonderful human
                  being?

Result: Arousal of doubt and concern
                  responses

Sample Data vs.
Belief Problems

Example #1

Student Belief: What you read in print must be
                  true or else it would not be in
                  print in the first place

Data
(from teacher):   Several instances of obviously
                  untrue material in printed form

Result: Arousal of doubt and concern
                  responses

Example #2

Student Belief: Any hard-working, ambitious Black
can get out of the ghetto
poverty cycle if he really wants
to do so

Data
(from teacher): Several true stories of ambitious, hard-working Blacks who
wanted to break the poverty
cycle, but were met with tremendous obstacles and frustrations
and consequently failed in their
attempts

Result: Arousal of doubt and concern
responses

In certain respects, the authentic problems approach is probably the most complex of the clarifying
strategies presented thus far. In order to be effective in utilizing the approach, the teacher must know
something about the beliefs and values of his students.
Also, by its very nature, the approach implies that
further investigation should follow (i.e., investigation into the nature of the problem in an attempt to
resolve the doubt and concern that has been generated).
Because of the differing ways students have learned to
deal with apparent inadequacies and consistencies in
their beliefs, the strategy will at times seem strongly
cognitive whereas at other times it will appear mainly
affective. In any event, if the strategy helps to
create problems of doubt and concern on the part of
students, it will have, in fact, revealed affective dispositions at several levels of the affective classification model.

A word of caution is appropriate at this point. The
authentic problems approach should not be used unless
it is followed by further investigation. No useful
purpose is served by leaving students with unresolved
doubts and concerns. The values and conflicts that
are revealed should be clarified further and consequently examined by means of value analysis or moral
reasoning strategies.

Clarifying Response Approach

A strategy designed to emphasize a personal frame-of-reference (see page 120) has been developed by Raths and his associates. It consists of a specific method or way for the teacher to respond to what students say or do. The strategy is based upon the Raths model of the process of valuing discussed in Chapter Three. According to Raths, a given belief, purpose, or attitude becomes a value for the individual only after it has progressed through the various phases of this process. The process is briefly summarized below:

The process used by the individual in developing his values includes choosing, prizing, and acting in the following schema:

Choosing:
1. Freely;
2. From alternatives;
3. After thoughtful consideration of the consequences of each alternative;

Prizing:
4. Cherishing, being happy with the choice;
5. Willing to affirm the choice publicly;

Acting:
6. Doing something with the choice;
7. Repeatedly, in some pattern of life.[8]

Using the various steps of the process model as a guide, the teacher interested in value clarification can pose probing questions designed to stimulate students to reflect upon what they have chosen, what they prize, or what they are doing. Raths summarizes the basic intent of the approach as follows:

The purpose of the clarifying response is to raise questions in the mind of the student, to prod him gently to examine his life, his actions, and his ideas, with the expectation that some will want to use this prodding as an opportunity to clarify their understandings, purposes, feelings, aspirations, attitudes, beliefs, and so on.[9]

Raths suggests that specific probing questions can be devised which are appropriate stimulators at each of the seven steps of the valuing process. The following questions are illustrative of the clarifying response approach (questions which can be utilized after the student has said or done something with affective overtones).

Questions for Each Step of the Valuing Process	Apparent Relationship to Affective Domain Classification Model
1. Questions related to choosing freely:	
a. Where do you suppose you first got that idea?	• Questions prompt thought first at the Reacting level and later at the Conforming level
b. How long have you felt that way?	
c. Are you the only one in your crowd who feels this way?	
d. What do your parents want you to do?	
e. Is there any rebellion in your choice?	
2. Questions related to choosing from alternatives:	
a. What else did you consider before you picked this?	• Questions move students from the Conforming to the Validating level
b. How long did you look around before you decided?	
c. Did you consider another possible alternative?	
d. Are there some reasons behind your choice?	
e. What choices did you reject before you settled on your present idea or action?	

130

3. Questions related to
choosing after consider-
ing consequences:

    a. What would be the con-   • Questions focus
        sequences of each   thought on the
        alternative available?   Validating process
    b. What assumptions are
        involved in your
        choice?
    c. Now if you do this,
        what will happen to
        that . . . ?
    d. Is what you say con-
        sistent with what
        you said earlier?
    e. Have you really
        weighed it fully?

4. Questions related to
prizing and cherishing:

    a. Are you glad you feel   • Questions could be used
        that way?   to prompt responses
    b. How long have you   related to either the
        wanted it?   Conforming or Validat-
    c. What good is it?   ing levels
        What purpose does it
        serve? Why is it
        important to you?
    d. Is it something you
        really prize?
    e. In what way would life
        be different without
        it?

5. Questions related to
prizing and affirming:

    a. Would you tell the   • Questions could be used
        class the way you feel   to determine whether
        some time?   students are operating
    b. Would you be willing   at Conforming or
        to sign a petition   Validating level
        supporting that idea?
    c. Should a person who
        believes the way you
        do speak out?

    d. Do people know that you
       believe that way or
       that you do that thing?
    e. Are you willing to
       stand up and be
       counted for that?

6. Questions related to
   acting upon choices:

    a. I hear what you are   • Questions related main-
       for; now, is there   ly to the Validating
       anything you can do   level (with perhaps a
       about it? Can I   hint of Affective
       help?   Judging at d and e)
    b. What are your first
       steps, second steps,
       and so on?
    c. Have you made any
       plans to do more than
       you already have done?
    d. Where will this lead
       you? How far are you
       willing to go?
    e. How has it already
       affected your life?
       How will it affect it
       in the future?

7. Questions related to
   acting repeatedly:

    a. Have you felt this   • Questions related
       way for some time?   mainly to the Validat-
    b. Have you done anything   ing level (with a
       already? Do you do   slight Affective Judg-
       this often?   ing orientation at d
    c. What are your plans   and e)
       for doing more of it?
    d. Are there some other
       things you can do which
       are like it?
    e. Will you do it again?[10]

        Raths suggests that the clarifying response can
be very effective when it is aimed at one student at a
time during informal teacher-student interchanges in
the hall, on the playground, or while participating in

132

school activities. The approach can also be developed along the lines of the value sheet exercise discussed earlier, with several students responding in writing and with subsequent discussion groups organized to further explore the ideas expressed. For crucial societal issues or ideas where the sharing of ideas is deemed to be important for all concerned, the approach might form the basis for class or small group discussions in which all students are encouraged to respond, but under no compulsion to do so. The ultimate purpose of the strategy is to afford the students an opportunity to think about and clarify their affective dispositions and values.

The clarifying response approach illustrates both the advantages and limitations of strategies based upon the Raths value process model. The process model can serve as the basis for many thought-provoking questions that can prompt students to view ideas and values from many perspectives. However, as noted above, the questions neglect the Affective Judging and Affective Creating levels. Although several levels are touched upon, the approach is rather general and does not provide clear guidelines for movement to higher affective levels. Strategies based upon the Raths model are largely diagnostic, descriptive, and open-ended, with little or no provision for involving students with new ideas (or values), helping them organize their value systems, or confronting them with value conflicts.

Cultural Value
System Approach

An approach oriented toward the frame-of-reference of other cultures or groups has been proposed for the social studies and related fields. The proposal is basically a curricular model wherein content is organized in such a way as to make the value-dimensions of human behavior the central focus. The concept of dominant value is suggested as the basic content organizer. The study of dominant value systems would become the core of the curriculum, thereby providing the basis for a unified social studies concerned with a subject matter common to a variety of academic disciplines. Even though the approach is intended more as a general curricular design rather than as a teaching strategy, the basic idea is suggestive of a number of teaching strategies that would lead students toward an

identification and clarification of feelings, attitudes, and values other than their own--and other than
those of their own culture or group. In supporting
what might be termed a dominant value curriculum, one
writer maintains that values are

> . . . the most distinctive characteristic
> of man. The most significant aspect of a
> social group is its dominant value system.
> A similarity of dominant values identifies
> the members of a social group and ought to
> be the first concern of any attempt to
> understand that group . . . it is just not
> possible to study all the values of a
> group, nor is it really necessary. The
> concept of dominant value narrows the con-
> tent to manageable proportions--those col-
> lectively held assumptions about and
> orientations toward the things that matter
> the most. This is the core of the social
> studies. It must be taught intentionally,
> specifically, and thoroughly.[11]

The basic components of a general curricular approach for guiding the study of dominant values in the
classroom is presented below. It recommends itself as
a useful means of organizing content and exploring the
value-dimensions of human behavior, past and present.
It includes seven elements or points of emphasis;
namely, dominant values, the creation of values, the
transmission of values, value change, value-related
prediction, value conflict, and the comparison of
values. The approach is described in more detail, and
with sample probing questions, in Appendix B.

1. Identifying and clarifying dominant values (of
   culture and/or subgroups);
2. Determining the factors that contributed to
   the creation of the dominant values;
3. Determining the means by which dominant values
   are transmitted from generation to generation;
4. Determining the contemporary influences (or
   factors) tending to change the dominant values;
5. Formulating predictive hypotheses about patterns of behavior;
6. Analyzing the nature of value conflicts;
7. Comparing cultural value systems (past and
   present).[12]

The approach can be used in several different ways. It can be employed in examining the dominant values of (1) entire cultures, (2) subgroups within cultures, or (3) particular individuals within subgroups of cultures. The first six elements--or topics--are largely cognitive, but with definite affective overtones. The probing questions presented in Appendix B are designed to promote a thorough investigation of the six topics, thereby involving students in the process of identifying and clarifying the feelings and values of many diverse cultures, groups, or individuals. The data collected will prompt a variety of Reacting and Conforming responses which can be further clarified and analyzed. The approach brings students into contact with a wealth of information about value dispositions both similar to and different from their own. This can provide the basis for comparisons with their own ideas and values. The final element--or topic--involves students in comparing values and in making hypothetical choices between particular values or value systems. Such activities will encourage Conforming and Validating responses and, on occasion, may stimulate Affective Judging. The experience should be helpful to students as they continue to clarify and develop their values.

Empathetic Approach

A final frame-of-reference for the clarifying process involves asking students to view an idea or situation from another person's vantage point; in essence, to engage in the vicarious experience of "trying to wear someone else's shoes for a while." In the process, students should begin to see more clearly the broad spectrum of human feelings and values, the similarities and differences between individual perspectives, and the range of alternatives that are available to them as they think about their own feelings and values. The empathetic approach requires students to think about and discuss the affective behaviors of others, but most important, they are asked to do this by placing themselves in the other person's place. Thus, students are also examining their own feelings and values. Continued and persistent practice in identifying, clarifying, and speculating about a variety of affective behaviors prepares the student (and may even serve as a stimulus) for involvement in thinking at the Validating level of the affective classification model.

What follows is a five-part teaching strategy designed to encourage students to empathize with other people who are faced with perplexing problems, or who display certain values or strong feelings.[13]

Describing

1. Students <u>introduced</u> to a real or fictional account of an individual in a rather difficult and/or emotional situation (usually involves some kind of a personal dilemma or a situation evoking strong emotions).

   a. Situation is <u>presented</u> by means of film, reading, or oral narration. General examples of types of situations might include the following:

      (1) Situation where someone is experiencing discrimination;
      (2) Situation where someone is ordered by a superior to do something that is contrary to his beliefs;
      (3) Situation where someone demonstrates loyalty and dedication to an idea or person(s) that the students strongly oppose or dislike.

   b. Students asked to <u>describe</u> the various aspects of the situation encountered.

Hypothesizing

2. Students asked to <u>hypothesize</u> about <u>how</u> they believe the person feels in the situation described.

3. Students asked to <u>hypothesize</u> about <u>why</u> the person feels as they say he does.

Analogous Experience and/or Role Playing

4. Students asked if they have found themselves in similar situations in the past, and if so . . .

4. Students asked to assume the role of person in the described situation, and then . . . .

137

(a) Describe how	(a) Describe how
they felt;	they would feel;
(b) Discuss why they	(b) Discuss why they
felt that way.	would feel that
	way.

Generalizing

5. Students asked to think in general terms about
    people in similar situations. Move toward
    possible generalization(s) about the feelings
    of people in such situations.

Although some clarifying strategies encourage
thinking at the Validating level and above, they do
not provide specific procedures and guidelines for the
kind of systematic investigation required at the higher
levels. However, such strategies do provide students
with many value-related experiences that can serve as
background preparation for the more sophisticated and
analytical processes involved in the value analysis
and moral reasoning strategies presented in the following sections.

VALUE ANALYSIS STRATEGIES

As indicated earlier, value analysis is a process
which emphasizes empirical analysis, testing, and practical application. It is basically a rational means
for appraising things in terms of their worth. Thus,
value analysis can be defined as a logical process by
which rational and defensible value decisions can be
made. Value analysis strategies are appropriate when
the teacher wishes his students to become involved in
an in-depth investigation of the worth of certain
positions, policies, or ideas (e.g., capital punishment, disarmament, abortion, environmental preservation, gun control, smoking, women's rights, pre-marital
sex, farm subsidies, and so on). Although such
strategies emphasize systematic thinking at the
Validating level, they also are designed to stimulate
thinking about relationships between values and potential value conflicts. Hence, in helping students to
develop and validate their value positions, value
analysis strategies prepare them for dealing with
values and value conflicts (or moral dilemmas) at the

Affective Judging level. In addition, a number of value analysis strategies prompt students to examine and relate various segments of their value systems, thereby moving them into the initial Affective Creating sublevel (Integrating Values).

A comprehensive and thorough treatment of value analysis as it relates to teaching may be found in Values Education: Rationale, Strategies, and Procedures, edited by L. E. Metcalf. The volume identifies three objectives for value analysis in a pedagogical setting, namely; (1) helping students make the most rational decisions they can make about value issues, (2) helping students develop the capabilities and dispositions required for making rational value decisions, and (3) teaching students how to resolve value conflict between themselves and other members of a group. Also, six tasks are enumerated which must be carried out in any value analysis strategy (or process):

1. Identifying and clarifying the value question;

2. Assembling (gathering and organizing) purported facts;

3. Assessing the truth of purported facts;

4. Clarifying the relevance of facts;

5. Arriving at a tentative value decision;

6. Testing the value principle implied in the decision.[14]

Value Analysis Model

Metcalf and his associates have developed a model which depicts the logical elements of value analysis, and may be utilized as the basis for developing teaching strategies. They suggest that the model may be used directly as a focus for discussions as students engage in value analysis activities and projects. The four basic elements of the model are summarized as follows.

The first element is the thing being evaluated, which usually is called the value object (VO). Literally anything can be evaluated, so that the

VO can be any content.

The second element is the term, the value term (VT), which is applied to the value object to make the value judgment. A wide variety of VTs are used--good, desirable, right, just, fair, advisable, and so on.

The third element is the description (D). In the description, characteristics of the VO relevant to the VT are given, such as origins, consequences, features, and so on.

The fourth element is the criterion (C), some rule or standard by which it is judged whether or not the VT applies to the VO. The D and C together support the value judgment.[15]

The four elements of the model and certain of the relationships between them are represented in the following diagram.

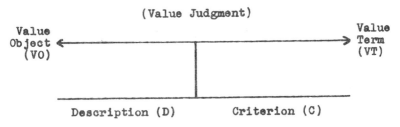

The upper horizontal line, an arrow, represents the application of the value term (VT) to the value object (VO), constituting the value judgment. The lower horizontal line over both the description (D) and the criterion (C) is to represent the fact that the description and criterion must both be present to provide support for the value judgment.

The Simple Value Model[16]
Figure 5

The following diagram is an illustration of the use of the model in dealing with a value judgment about air pollution. In this case, "air pollution" becomes the value object (VO), and the value term (VT) is "undesirable." The complete value judgment is then, "Air pollution is undesirable." In this instance, the description (D) is "Air pollution contributes to emphysema," and the criterion (C) is "Any condition which contributes to emphysema is undesirable."

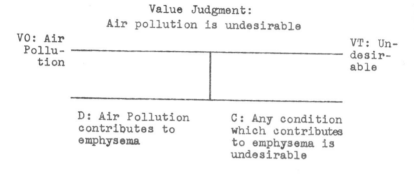

Value Judgment:
Air pollution is undesirable

VO: Air Pollution

VT: Undesirable

D: Air Pollution contributes to emphysema

C: Any condition which contributes to emphysema is undesirable

Example of the Use of the Simple Value Model in Evaluating Air Pollution[17]

Figure 6

The authors admit that the four elements as presented amount to a somewhat idealized version of the evaluative process. However, they do present an extended version of the model which involves more than one VO, more than one VT, and allows for a number of D-C combinations. The model is designed primarily to bring into focus the logical elements involved in the process of value analysis. The actual classroom application of the model would involve the development and use of teaching strategies designed to accomplish the six value analysis tasks enumerated earlier. Such strategies should move students from their initial Reacting and Conforming responses to serious involvement with Validating tasks, and ultimately toward relating their tested value positions with previously accepted values.

Jurisprudential Approach

A curriculum project based at Harvard University
developed materials and procedures designed to teach
high school students to clarify and justify their positions on important societal issues. The basic elements
of their approach include (1) the analysis of basic
issues in terms of moral-value, definitional, and fact-
explanation issues, (2) the use of distinct strategies
for justification and clarification of student views on
issues, and (3) the use of discussion processes in dealing with issues. As a guide for analyzing the dimensions
of issues to be investigated, they developed the following logical schema.[18]

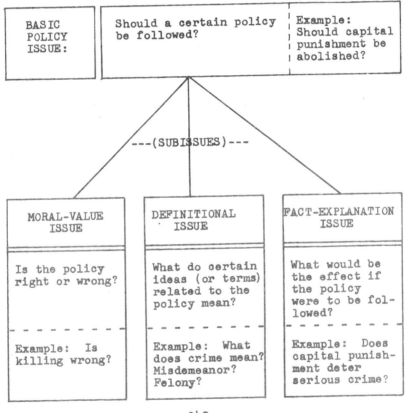

The project also developed a general strategy for the analysis of issues. It consists of a set of intellectual operations, listed in rough logical order below.

1. Abstracting general values from concrete situations;

2. Using general value concepts as dimensional constructs;

3. Identifying conflicts between value constructs;

4. Identifying a class of value conflict situations;

5. Discovering or creating value conflict situations which are analogous to the problem under discussion;

6. Working toward a general qualified position;

7. Testing the factual assumptions behind a qualified value decision;

8. Testing the relevance of statements.[19]

The project placed considerable emphasis on the case-study method (i.e., analogous cases) as a means of encouraging students to discuss and analyze the persisting human dilemmas related to contemporary issues and problems. They maintain that one of the most powerful techniques for dealing with value-related issues is to suggest that an issue might be resolved differently in several analogous cases. Their materials include detailed guidelines for the organization and stimulation of productive value-oriented discussions.

The jurisprudential approach contains the essential elements associated with value analysis, but with special emphasis on moral issues and analogous value conflicts. Thus, the approach moves the student toward a consideration of situations and circumstances in which Affective Judging is appropriate (and, on occasion, may stimulate thought on the Affective Creating level).

Heuristic Evaluative Model

Teachers serious about encouraging students to examine the validity of their beliefs need to develop teaching strategies designed specifically to involve them in analyzing and testing value judgments. The students must become familiar with specific analytical skills and subsequently afforded opportunities to practice using the skills with reference to particular value-laden ideas and issues. In the process, students will learn how to justify their value-positions, but also they can become aware of inconsistencies and incongruities in the way they support their beliefs, thus leading to value conflicts and frequent reassessments of what they value. Such an undertaking is no doubt rather ambitious for both teacher and student. It requires objectivity, persistence, tolerance for ambiguity, and special attention to the process of logical justification.

The evaluative model which is presented in Figure 7 consists of a set of general specifications intended to serve as a guide for the teacher--a basic framework within which the analysis and testing of value judgments can proceed. It makes explicit the direction in which the teacher should move and points out a number of important things which he should consider as he proceeds. In certain respects, the approach is similar to the previously discussed value analysis model developed by Metcalf and his associates.

Each major subdivision of the model represents a distinct stage in the evaluative process. The schematic diagram in Figure 7 provides a general overview; this is supplemented by a summary (including examples) of each phase or step of the model. A more detailed description of the model, along with sample probing questions and evaluations, is presented in Appendix C.

Summary of Steps in Model[21]	Example
(A) Phenomenon (i.e., clarification step)--At this step the phenomenon or thing to be evaluated is introduced and described (or defined). It is important that	• Dropping of atomic bomb on Hiroshima in 1945

(A) PHENOMENON
(Behavior, event, policy, object, or state of affairs being evaluated)

(B) APPRAISAL OR PRESCRIPTION

(1) Appraisal: The way the phenomenon is rated or graded. Such as: A-B-C-D-F; Good-Fair-Poor; Desirable-Undesirable; 1st rate-2nd rate-3rd rate; Good-Bad; Beautiful-Ugly

(2) Prescription: The way the phenomenon is judged with reference to possible action or behavior. Such as: injunctions, admonitions, oughts-ought nots, shoulds-should nots

(C) WARRANT (or justification) for Appraisal or Prescription

(1) Statement of Specific Warrant: Basically a statement of the (a) criteria (or rules), or (b) consequences, or (c) preferences, which are used to support, back up, or justify the appraisal or prescription

(2) Testing of Warrant(s):

(a) Criterial: Determine fit or consistency of phenomenon with specific criteria (or rules)

(b) Consequential: Determine whether or not phenomenon will produce or be followed by certain consequences

(c) Preferential: Determine fit or consistency of phenomenon with judger's life-style, character, and self concept

(D) GENERALIZED EVALUATION

(1) Formulation of generalized statement of evaluation (combining appraisal or prescription and tested warrant):

Form: "All phenomena warranted (or justified) in this way are to be appraised or prescribed in this way."

(2) Application of generalized evaluation:

(a) Instances of other phenomena that fit (or conform to) the warrant are presented

(b) Determine whether or not the student is inclined to employ the same appraisal or prescription to such phenomena

Heuristic Evaluative Model[20]

Figure 7

145

students know exactly what it is
they are to evaluate.

(B) <u>Appraisal</u> or <u>Prescription</u> (i.e.,
<u>reactions to the phenomenon</u>)--At
this step students are asked to
<u>react</u> to the phenomenon by offer-
ing appraisals (approve-disap-
prove, for example) or prescriptions (oughts-ought nots, for
example). The various appraisals
and prescriptions are noted and
become the focus of the next step.

- The atomic
  bomb should
  <u>not</u> have been
  dropped (nega-
  tive prescrip-
  tion)

(C) <u>Warrant</u> or <u>Justification</u> (i.e.,
reasons for reactions stated and
tested)--At this step the students
are asked for <u>reasons</u> (warrants)
for the appraisals or prescriptions
offered in the previous step.
Subsequently, the reasons are
classified as: (a) criterial or
rule reasons, (b) consequential
reasons, or (c) preferential (intrinsic) reasons.

- The dropping of
  the atomic bomb
  resulted in the
  death of more
  civilians than
  military per-
  sonnel
- (The above is a
  consequential
  reason-warrant)

Each reason (warrant) is tested
for its validity in the appropriate fashion: whether criteria or rules fit phenomenon;
whether consequences follow
phenomenon; or whether judger
is being internally consistent.
All reasons (warrants) that are
validated can be used in the
final step below.

- Empirical test-
  ing by referring
  to available
  data on the
  subject
- (The above con-
  sequence tests
  out as valid)

(D) <u>Generalized</u> Evaluation (i.e.,
generalizing tested warrants to
other situations)--At this step
each appraisal (or prescription)
is combined with its tested
warrant and converted into a
generalized value statement.

- <u>All</u> military
  weapons (or
  tactics) that
  result in the
  death of more
  civilians than
  military person-
  nel should <u>not</u>
  be used

Subsequently, the teacher suggests similar situations and

- Would you eval-
  uate the

asks students if they are willing to apply their evaluation in the same way. This step remains open-ended, and the students may agree, disagree, or choose to re-examine their positions and go through the process again, using a phenomenon from one of the examples.

Additional examples are included in Appendix C.

- fire-bombing of German cities during World War II in the same way?
- Would you evaluate the siege of Vicksburg during the Civil War in the same way?
- Would you evaluate the use of germ warfare (after an atomic attack on the U.S.) in the same way?

Although the model emphasizes thinking at the Validating level, it prompts students to move progressively through the first five levels of the affective classification model. On occasion, it will stimulate thought at the Affective Creating level. Step A of the model is largely cognitive, even though unsolicited Reacting and Conforming responses may occur in the process. Step B will elicit a variety of Reacting and Conforming responses. Step C, the heart of the model, is initiated by Conforming level thinking, but the ultimate intent is to force the student to validate his position(s) by means of empirical and logical analysis. When students become involved in formulating and applying generalized evaluations at step D, they may begin to operate at the Affective Judging level. In dealing with generalized evaluations, students ponder how broadly they are willing to apply particular value positions, and hence, are forced to think about the degree to which they are consistent in their valuing and how their values are related to one another. This task may reveal inconsistencies and value conflicts that will prompt them to engage in thinking at the Affective Judging level and at the Integrating Values sublevel of Affective Creating.

MORAL REASONING STRATEGIES

Moral reasoning strategies focus upon thinking at both subcategories of the Affective Judging level

147

(i.e., 5.1--Establishing Value Criteria and 5.2--Value Judging), and at the first sublevel of Affective Creating (i.e., 6.1--Integrating Values). The ultimate purpose of such strategies is to involve students in an introspective examination of their total value structures (or systems). From the 5.1--Value Criteria perspective, the strategies should focus student attention on the task of developing specific value criteria which can serve as the basis for ordering and making choices between values. From the 5.2--Value Judging perspective, moral reasoning strategies should confront students with value dilemmas that force them to use their established value criteria in making choices between certain accepted values. From the 6.1--Integrating perspective, such strategies should prompt students to organize, classify, and relate their accepted values, value criteria, and value judgments in terms of similarities and differences and with reference to the types of circumstances in which they are most appropriate. In addition, students should have opportunities (if so inclined) to re-examine the appropriateness of the criteria they employ in making choices in conflict situations. Ultimately, moral reasoning strategies should encourage serious consideration of how consistent and logical student value systems are, and how workable they are in dealing with day-to-day experiences.

Several of the value analysis strategies presented in the previous section encourage students to think about developing value criteria (see in particular the Criterion component of the Metcalf Value Analysis Model and the Generalized Evaluation section of the Heuristic Evaluative Model). Special strategies can be developed that are designed to promote thinking at each sublevel discussed above (5.1, 5.2, and 6.1). However, in this section, a single strategy will be discussed that focuses mainly on the Value Judging and Integrating Values sublevels (with attention to Establish-Value Criteria as appropriate). The strategy will be preceded by a discussion of a theory or moral development.

Value-conflicts and the
Theory of Moral Development

When students are confronted with value-conflicts they are in a situation where they must choose between "goods." That is, they are forced to make a choice between two or more high priority values. In a very real sense, such a conflict (or dilemma) amounts to a direct challenge to the student's system of values--it might be termed "value-shock." Not only are two or more discrete values at issue, but the integrity of the entire value system is at stake. Somehow, the student must be able to justify his ultimate choice between "goods" in a way that is consistent with the way his value system has been developed, organized, and ordered. Through the experience of developing a value system and of confronting earlier dilemmas, the student will have developed a response pattern to conflict situations. In short, the student will have evolved a type of affective set that comes into play whenever he is faced with value conflicts (moral dilemmas). Such response patterns or affective sets are merely another way of describing what the affective domain classification model identifies as established value criteria (i.e., the criterial base and orientation for ordering and choosing between accepted values). Thus, depending upon the nature of a person's personal experience (and the extent of his value development), a particular response or value criterion can be classified at one of the following levels of moral judgment or reasoning (based upon Kohlberg's theory of moral reasoning): Pre-conventional Level; Conventional Level; and Principled Level.[22]

1. Pre-conventional Level--Where the individual responds to a value-conflict (moral dilemma) in terms of the cultural rules and labels of good and bad, right or wrong. He interprets the rules and labels in terms of possible physical or hedonistic consequences (such as punishment, reward, exchange of favors), or in terms of the physical power or prestige of those whom he identifies with the rules and labels. This level is divided into two developmental stages:

    Stage #1: Obedience and Punishment Orientation;

    Stage #2: Instrumental Relativisitic Orientation.

2. Conventional Level--Where the individual responds to a value-conflict (moral dilemma)

by taking the view that maintaining, supporting, and conforming to the expectations of
family, group, or nation is valuable in its
own right, regardless of the consequences to
his own immediate and obvious needs. The
individual is not only concerned with conformity, but also with the demonstration of
his loyalty through actively supporting and
justifying orderliness and stability in the
group. He identifies with the group and its
members and perceives that his moral choices
must conform to the expectations of the group.
This level is divided into two developmental
stages:

Stage #3: Interpersonal Sharing Orientation;

Stage #4: Societal Maintenance Orientation.

3. Principled Level--Where the individual responds
to a value-conflict (moral dilemma) by becoming
involved in a conscious effort to identify and
clarify moral values and principles which have
validity and general applicability apart from
the authority of the groups or persons holding
the values, and apart from the individual's own
identification with such groups or individuals.
This level is divided into two developmental
stages:

Stage #5: Social-contract, Human Rights and
Welfare Orientation;

Stage #6: Universal Ethical Principle Orientation.

Based on Kohlberg's developmental stages, established value criteria can be thought of as affective
stage orientations of six different types (i.e., stage
1 value criteria, stage 2 value criteria, and so on).
Thus, when individuals are confronted with value-
conflicts (dilemmas), the type of value criteria they
utilize in attempting to resolve the dilemma reflects
their current stage of moral development.

According to Kohlberg, individuals in all cultures
go through the sequence of stages in their moral development.[23] However, this does not mean that all persons
achieve stage 6, since anyone can become "fixated" at

any stage. Further, since the stages are developmental in nature, it is not possible to skip stages, although some people move more quickly through the stages than do others.

Although the same person _may_ use different stages at different times, most people are relatively consistent. Thus, at any given time it is possible to identify a person's predominant stage of reasoning by matching his reactions to a moral dilemma with the appropriate stage characteristics. (Of course, the novice may experience initial difficulty in determining stage classifications. See Appendix D for a more detailed description of the Kohlberg levels and stages of moral development.)

It is important to remember that the stages are "affective orientations" (or points of view) and not merely a series of specific choices. There is a stage 1 orientation (or point of view), a stage 2 orientation, and so forth, with respect to given types of values and issues (e.g., property, law, life, liberty, and so forth). Even though individuals at any stage may choose any position on a given moral dilemma, the rationale (or warrant or value criteria) they employ in support of the position will be dependent upon their stage of moral development. Thus, individuals choosing the same position may support the position with different rationales.

The following findings and conclusions of Kohlberg and his associates have important implications for educational practice:

1. Young people who operate at stages 5 and 6 are more likely to act justly (i.e., consider the rights of others);

2. Young people tend to _prefer_ the highest level or moral reasoning that they can comprehend;

3. Young people are able to understand all stages below their own and often one or more above their own;

4. When young people come to understand the stage immediately above their own, they tend to prefer it to their own stage;

5. Young people advance more rapidly through the sequence of stages when they have frequent opportunities to engage in serious discussions of moral dilemmas with their peers.[24]

These conclusions have led to the development of a model designed to assist teachers who are interested in involving their students in activities likely to facilitate movement from stage to stage. Use of the model is possible without the necessity of intensive study, on the part of the teacher, of complex procedures for classifying each student at the appropriate stage of moral development.

Teaching Model for Moral Development

As indicated earlier, Kohlberg views moral reasoning as a developmental process. Individuals move consecutively from stage to stage, progressing toward broader, more flexible ways of viewing moral problems (i.e., they tend to change their established value criteria as they grow and experience life). If the teacher wishes to facilitate the movement of pupils from stage to stage, he will need to utilize teaching strategies whereby students will be (1) confronted with moral dilemmas, (2) encouraged to discuss and exchange views about the dilemmas, and (3) exposed to moral reasoning at a stage above their own. Further, the above activities should take place in a setting or "climate" that is supportive and nonthreatening to the student. A set of teaching strategies consistent with the above specifications is outlined in Figure 8.

The teaching model includes five steps which can serve as a guide to the teacher as he involves students in learning activities related to a given moral dilemma. The search questions are intended to illustrate the general focus and purpose of each step in the model.

The model can be utilized whenever a moral dilemma is suggested or implied by the usual content of a course and/or whenever students have special concerns or problems that appear to have the dimensions of a moral dilemma. Also, fictional dilemmas may be employed that are illustrative of important social problems or issues. In general, the moral dilemmas should be built around the series of universal moral issues

(1) FOCUSING ON DILEMMA ────────→ (2) SPECIFYING POSITIONS

   Search Question:
   What is the moral
   dilemma?
   (See example)

   (Full class presentation
   and discussion)

Search Question:
What should be done
about the dilemma?

(Full class discus-
sion)

(4) EXPLORING ALTERNATIVES ←──── (3) SPECIFYING WARRANTS

   Search Questions:
   What are other views
   about what should be
   done? How are views
   backed up?

   (Full class presentations
   from groups and discussion)

Search Question:
Why should it be
done?

(Small group discus-
sions where the stu-
dents are mixed on
all variables excep'
that of position
taken)

(5) EVALUATION

   Search Question:
   What does this dilemma
   and this moral reasoning
   experience mean to me?

   (Full class discussion and
   individual reflection)

The Gray Teaching Model for Moral Reasoning[25]

Figure 8

identified by Kohlberg: punishment, property, affection, authority, law, life, liberty, distributive justice, and truth. A sample moral dilemma is described below.

Harold's Dilemma

Harold is a serious-minded, hard-working family man. For years he received little recognition for his efforts. Ten years ago he took a new job and over that period he has been deeply appreciated and rewarded by his new boss. His boss has helped and encouraged him in his work, and even loaned him money when his wife was seriously ill. Harold now holds a good position and he has a boss he likes and respects.

In connection with his work, Harold recently came upon some information that provides proof that his boss has been cheating on his federal income taxes (about $15,000 over a period of five years). Harold is called upon to testify before a grand jury investigating his boss's tax returns. He is asked specifically whether or not he knows of any illegal acts of his boss relative to his tax returns.

Dilemma: Honesty vs. friendship
(What should Harold do, and why so?)

The teaching model which appears on page 153 is presented in detail below. Each reasoning step is described and then followed by a set of suggested teaching behaviors (or strategies). The model also provides sample student responses and reactions.

The student interactions at step 3 of the model are crucial for the developmental process. The purpose of the grouping is to facilitate student exposure to different stages of moral reasoning. At step 3 students should meet with a group, all of whom have taken the same position, but at the same time do not all hold the same warrant (or rationale) for the position. Students are thereby confronted with views on their position that are both alike and different from their own. It is important that this type of confrontation take place in the groups and, in particular, that students are exposed to reasoning at a higher stage than their own.

154

THE GRAY TEACHING MODEL FOR MORAL REASONING

REASONING STEPS	TEACHER BEHAVIORS	STUDENT BEHAVIORS
(1) FOCUSING ON DILEMMA Conflicting values brought into sharp focus by means of a moral dilemma (see Harold's Dilemma above)	Presents and/or reviews appropriate background information, etc. Presents dilemma Clarifies terminology, circumstances, and issues Solicits students' feedback	Receives information Asks informational and clarifying questions Demonstrates comprehension by defining, describing, or summarizing
(2) SPECIFYING POSITIONS Identification of initial reactions or conclusions regarding what should be done to resolve the moral dilemma. Recommended behavior or action is delineated	Solicits student positions Probes for clarification of positions Summarizes	Responds with position(s) regarding what should be done Responds by summarizing and elaborating on position(s) Receives information
(3) SPECIFYING WARRANTS Identification of the specific types of reasoning (or rationale) behind the positions that	Divides class into two or more groups of pupils who took the same position on the dilemma (groups should be generally	Receives information and instructions

155

REASONING STEPS	TEACHER BEHAVIOR	STUDENT BEHAVIOR
have been given (e.g., a <u>warrant</u> is a statement that specifies why a position was taken; the reasons or support for a position) NOTE: Identifying the warrant (rationale) amounts to specifying the established value criteria	heterogeneous in all respects except for positions taken on the dilemma) Instructs groups to: 1. List all warrants offered by group members; 2. Clarify all individual warrants offered; 3. Plan how to present warrants to full class; and 4. Compare and contrast warrants of group members. Circulates among groups encouraging listing of all warrants and stimulating interactions among group members	Participates in group discussion (receives and responds): Contributes own warrant to group list; Clarifies own warrant; Asks others to clarify; Works with group to plan presentation to class; Suggests similarities and differences between warrants.
(4) <u>EXPLORING ALTERNATIVES</u> Identification and comparison of different position-warrant combinations NOTE: Position A might have three different warrants (1, 2, 3) and	Asks groups to present lists Asks individuals to clarify and defend different position-warrant combinations Solicits the identification of similarities and differences	Receives instructions and presents lists Responds by clarifying and defending own position-warrant combination Responds by identifying similarities and

156

REASONING STEPS	TEACHER BEHAVIOR	STUDENT BEHAVIOR
Position B might also have three (4, 5, 6). In such a case, the position-warrant combinations would be A(1), A(2), A(3), and B(4), B(5), B(6)	between position-warrant combinations	differences between position-warrant combinations
(5) EVALUATION Evaluation procedures and activities would include the following: Summary of class reasoning; Individual evaluations (of own reasoning); Review of thinking processes employed; Evaluation of total experience.	Solicits summation of reasoning observed Encourages reflection and re-thinking relative to individual reasoning (non-threat, support-ive climate/ no consensus sought!) Solicits (or pre-sents) listing of steps in the process of moral reasoning Asks what was learned from moral reasoning experience	Responds with own perspective or summary Responds with judgments about own reasoning or with changed mode of reasoning (optional) Receives and/or offers list of steps Evaluates total experience

If, at first, the groups do not appear to have an adequate "mix" of different stages, the teacher will have to effect appropriate changes as the discussions progress.

How does the teacher ensure that proper groupings are made? The ideal procedure would be to pre-assess the exact stage of moral reasoning for each pupil and then group them accordingly. Unfortunately, Kohlberg's measuring instruments are currently rather complex and may be difficult for most teachers to utilize without in-service efforts. A workable alternative is to place a generally heterogeneous mix of students in each group--that is, in terms of intelligence, achievement, socio-economic background, and so on--then monitor the group discussions and make changes which seem necessary to bring about balance (based on the use of the stage definitions and sample stage warrants presented in Appendix D). Over a period of time, the teacher will become skillful in achieving a mix of stages within each group. Presently only a few teaching aids are available for teachers interested in moral development.[26]

The purpose of the moral reasoning teaching model is to confront students with moral dilemmas in such a way as to prompt them to think about their own reasoning and the reasoning of their peers. Involvement in the process affords them opportunities to gain new perspectives and to consider the possibility of adopting a higher stage of moral reasoning. When engaged in such activities, students are operating at the Affective Judging and Affective Creating levels of the affective domain classification model; they are moving back and forth between the Value Judging and Integrating Values sublevels and, on occasion, may initiate changes in their established value criteria.

STRATEGIES FOR ACTIVATING THE CREATIVE IMAGINATION

As indicated in Chapter Three, thinking at the Affective Creating level is related to the functioning of the creative imagination. An activated imagination is important, whether the individual is working toward a reorganized and more fully integrated system of values (6.1), or is searching for unique insights about values and valuing (6.2).

The Value Analysis and Moral Reasoning strategies discussed previously are likely to activate the creative imagination in such a way as to promote the integration of values (6.1). Unfortunately, there are very few teaching strategies designed to stimulate inspirational insights (6.2). However, there appear to be at least three specific things teachers can do to improve the chances of creative thinking among their students. First, teaching strategies should be employed that are designed to achieve a variety of higher-level cognitive and affective objectives. Second, a learning environment should be created wherein students are confronted with value-related problems of concern to them, and in which the "climate" is supportive, nonthreatening, rewarding, and ideationally diverse. Third, special teaching techniques should be utilized that have been found helpful in triggering the creative imagination and inspirational insights.

One of the more promising approaches in the field of creativity is known as Synectics. It includes a set of techniques for promoting creative thought by the use of metaphor. The Synectics method attempts to draw the individual into certain conscious, pre-conscious, and subconscious psychological states (e.g., empathy, involvement, play, detachment, and use of irrelevance) that are deemed prerequisites or necessary conditions for creative thinking. In order to move the individual into the psychological states, the Synectics approach suggests certain analytical procedures for making the strange familiar and a set of metaphorical mechanisms for making the familiar strange (e.g., Personal Analogy, Direct Analogy, Symbolic Analogy, and Fantasy Analogy).[27]

Once again it must be emphasized that at the higher levels of the classification model the three domains tend to merge together; consequently, the dividing lines between the three domains become increasingly indistinct. Hence, objectives, strategies, and learning activities that the teacher may develop for one learning domain may very well activate thinking or action in another domain.

159

ENDNOTES

[1]Detailed discussions of such goals and values are
to be found in Jack R. Fraenkel, Helping Students Think
and Value (Englewood Cliffs, New Jersey: Prentice-
Hall, Inc., 1973), pp. 254-62; and in Edwin Fenton,
Teaching the New Social Studies: An Inductive Approach
(New York: Holt, Rinehart and Winston, 1966), pp. 42-
45.

[2]Byron G. Massialas and C. Benjamin Cox, Inquiry
in Social Studies (New York: McGraw-Hill Book Company,
Inc., 1966), p. 175.

[3]Louis E. Raths, Merrill Harmin, and Sidney Simon,
Values and Teaching (Columbus, Ohio: Charles E.
Merrill, 1966), pp. 83-111.

[4]Ibid., pp. 104-05, and 231-32.

[5]Sidney B. Simon, "Values-Clarification vs.
Indoctrination," Social Education, 35 (December 1971):
902-05, 915.

[6]Fraenkel, Helping Students Think and Value, p.
235.

[7]This approach is adapated from ideas presented in
the following works: Charles E. Gray, et al., A
Portrait of Change: Teacher's Guide (Springfield,
Illinois: Sixth Illinois Constitutional Convention,
1970); and Maurice P. Hunt and Lawrence E. Metcalf,
Teaching High School Social Studies (New York: Harper
and Row, Publishers, 1968), pp. 72-74.

[8]Raths, Harmin, and Simon, Values and Teaching,
p. 30.

[9]Ibid., p. 80.

[10]Sample questions adapted from chart appearing in
ibid., pp. 63-65.

[11] Marion Brady, "The Key Concept," _Social Educa-tion_, 33 (November 1967):601.

[12] Categories adapted from ideas suggested in ibid., and from a related teaching model appearing in Charles E. Gray, "Value Inquiry and the Social Studies," _Educa-tion_, 93 (November-December 1972):130-37.

[13] A somewhat similar strategy for exploring feel-ings was developed as part of the Taba Curriculum Development Project at San Francisco State College. See Hilda Taba, et al., _A Teacher's Handbook to Ele-mentary Social Studies_ (Menlo Park, California: Addison-Wesley Publishing Company, 1971), pp. 76-80.

[14] Jerrold R. Coombs and Milton Meux, "Teaching Strategies for Value Analysis," in _Values Education: Rationale, Strategies and Procedures_, ed. Lawrence E. Metcalf (Washington, D.C.: National Council for the Social Studies, 1971), p. 29.

[15] James Chadwick and Milton Meux, "Procedures for Value Analysis," in _Values Education: Rationale, Strategies and Procedures_, ed. Lawrence E. Metcalf (Washington, D.C.: National Council for the Social Studies, 1971), pp. 81-82.

[16] Ibid., p. 82.

[17] Ibid., p. 83.

[18] Adapted from Donald W. Oliver and Fred M. Newmann, _Taking a Stand_ (Columbus, Ohio: American Edu-cation Publications, 1967), pp. 29-37. See also, Fred M. Newman, _Clarifying Public Controversy_ (Boston: Little, Brown and Company, 1970), p. 43.

[19] Donald W. Oliver and James P. Shaver, _Teaching Public Issues in the High School_ (Boston: Houghton Mifflin Company, 1966), pp. 126-30.

[20]Charles E. Gray, "Curricular and Heuristic Models for Value Inquiry," Paper presented at the College and University Faculty Assembly of the National Council for the Social Studies Convention, Boston, November 1972, p. 13 (ERIC Document 070737).

[21]Adapted from ibid., pp. 9-12, 19-26, and from Gray, "Value Inquiry and the Social Studies."

[22]Adapted from discussions of the Kohlberg theory and research appearing in the following: Lawrence Kohlberg and Carol Gilligan, "The Adolescent as a Philosopher: The Discovery of the Self in a Post-Conventional World," Daedalus, 100 (Fall 1971):1051-86; Lawrence Kohlberg, "The Child as a Moral Philosopher," Psychology Today, 7 (1968):25-30; Lawrence Kohlberg and Moshe M. Blatt, "The Effects of Classroom Moral Discussion Upon Children's Level of Moral Judgment," in Recent Research in Moral Development, eds. Lawrence Kohlberg and E. Turiel (Cambridge, Massachusetts: Moral Education and Research Foundation, 1974), Chapter Thirty-eight; and Lawrence Kohlberg, "The Cognitive-Developmental Approach to Moral Education," Phi Delta Kappan, 61 (June 1975):670-77.

[23]The discussion of Kohlberg's theory is based largely on the foregoing citations and on an edited compendium; Charles E. Gray, "The Theory of Moral Development: Meanings, Implications, and Applications for Teaching" (unpublished paper, 1975), 15 p.

[24]The conclusions are summarized in the edited compendium cited above, pp. 6-7.

[25]The teaching model for moral reasoning was originally presented in Charles E. Gray, "The Theory of Moral Development: Meanings, Implications, and Applications for Teaching" (unpublished paper, 1975), pp. 7-13. The April 1976 issue of Social Education, vol. 40, contains a special section on Kohlberg's theory and its applications in the classroom. It is one of the most comprehensive (and readable) presentations of the subject currently available. A teaching strategy is also included in the special section.

[26]James Rest of the University of Minnesota has
developed an instrument for measuring moral stage
development. It is known as the <u>Defining Issues Test</u>,
and can be obtained from him through the Department of
Psychology, University of Minnesota, Minneapolis,
Minnesota. Lawrence Kohlberg and Edwin Fenton have
developed a set of materials for use in in-service
workshops for teachers who wish to learn how to conduct
moral discussions. The materials are, <u>Learning to Lead
Moral Discussion: A Teacher Preparation Kit</u> (Pleasant-
ville, New York: Guidance Associates, 1976). Another
recent monograph is: Edwin Fenton, <u>The Implications of
Lawrence Kohlberg's Research for Civic Education.</u> It
is a preliminary draft of a paper being prepared for
the Institute for Developmental Educational Activities
of the Charles F. Kettering Foundation. It is available from the authors in mimeographed form.

[27]William J. J. Gordon, <u>Synectics</u> (New York:
Harper and Row, Publishers, 1961). See, in particular,
Chapters One and Two.

CHAPTER VII--Strategies in the Use
of the Psychomotor Domain

In contrast to consistent efforts to
analyze teaching that have been made in the cognitive
and affective domains, the psychomotor domain has received only fragmented attention. As a consequence,
a massive dependence upon a single teaching strategy
has developed. This strategy is the demonstration.
Because the demonstration lesson finds its best use at
the Activating-Executing (lower) levels, this in turn
has helped perpetuate the notion that learning in the
psychomotor domain is inferior to learning in the cognitive domain.

This chapter will present ways in which
the classification model for the psychomotor domain may
be applied, as well as examine each level in the
psychomotor model for useful teaching strategies.

OBJECTIVE, ACTIVITY, AND EVALUATION
CORRESPONDENCE

The teacher in a teaching area that emphasizes psychomotor skills is both the recipient and the
victim of a characteristic of the psychomotor domain as
content. Since many of the skills to be learned are at
the Activating and Executing levels, the behaviors are
easily defined and quickly understood by the students.
Thus the problem of powerfully communicating instructional intent that is encountered in the other two
domains has been minimized. This is true because in
the psychomotor domain that which is to be learned is

a behavior. In the other two domains, that which is to be learned is often an intellectual operation or affective response represented by a behavior.

Thus, teachers working in the psychomotor domain have found it relatively easy to achieve correspondence between their objectives, learning activities, and evaluations at the lower psychomotor levels. For instance, it does not take a great deal of effort to discern that being able to drill a hole properly in a piece of wood with a hand drill demands practice at drilling such a hole. Ultimately the production of a piece of wood with a smooth hole in it is used to demonstrate competence.

The irony of the situation, however, is that many teachers do not understand why students fail to grasp and achieve teacher objectives that are hazily conceived at the Maneuvering and Performance Judging levels. Even when the teacher can define precisely the objective (for instance, to achieve maneuverability in the choice of tools when constructing a project) the emphasis often remains on the quality of the final product and overshadows the maneuvers used to produce it.

NEGLECT OF HIGHER PSYCHOMOTOR LEVELS

In the cognitive domain, there is sufficient awareness of the existence of intellectual levels so that teachers who teach only for retention may be called to task. In the psychomotor domain, there is not nearly as much indignation when students have not been assisted to move beyond the Activating and Executing levels. The psychomotor domain is viewed by many as consisting solely of psychomotor Perceiving, Activating, and Executing.

Fortunately, there are also many teachers who consistently encourage students to try new ways to accomplish the same results, develop new products, and involve students in the evaluation of them. The problem is that by far the vast majority of these efforts are a product of incidental movements rather than precise planning and objective writing. Properly used, the teacher can utilize the psychomotor domain classification scheme to ensure a balance in psychomotor levels.

USING THE PSYCHOMOTOR CLASSIFICATION
MODEL IN PLANNING

Teachers familiar with this classification model can utilize it to generate sets of objectives in any particular area of content to ensure coverage of a variety of levels. This is directly analogous to the process described in Chapter Five, "Strategies for the Use of the Cognitive Domain." First, the teacher identifies the psychomotor skills the student must be able to demonstrate. These are then modeled by the students until they can be Executed. For instance, this identification may yield the objective "The student will be able to splice, solder, and cover 14-gauge copper wires to meet the electrical code standards." At the Activating level, the student will model each subsection (splicing, soldering, and covering) until he achieves ability at the Executing level.

At the Maneuvering level, the teacher may generate such objectives as "Given a terminal box and final product specifications, the student will select and execute necessary wiring connections that will meet electrical code standards."

Further, "After inspecting two houses during construction, the student will judge which of the two houses' electrical circuitry is (1) better in design, and (2) better in quality of workmanship, citing reasons for his judgments." Thus each objective moves up in levels, culminating in a Judging level objective.

PSYCHOMOTOR LEVELS AND STRATEGIES

Whereas in the cognitive domain there are many commonly used teaching strategies that can be analyzed in terms of their relationship to differing intellectual levels, there are few widely accepted counterparts in the psychomotor domain. It therefore seems expedient to examine each level in the psychomotor domain individually in order to identify practices and suggest strategies.

PSYCHOMOTOR
PERCEIVING-ACTIVATING

Early Childhood Education,
Psychomotor Perceiving
and Activating

In early childhood education, a major portion of
teacher effort is directed toward assisting students in
sensory and motor development. Current efforts in preparing teachers to gain competencies in this area
include emphasis on topics such as child-oriented
spontaneous movements, rhythmic activity programs,
whole body movements, kinesthetic awareness, and auditory perception games.

A typical work in this area is that of Clare
Cherry,[1] who has assembled a list of movements used by
children. The list includes: (1) body movements,
(2) hand and arm movements, (3) finger movements, and
(4) leg and foot movements. In all, over seventy
identifiable activities are noted. Such classifications are useful devices for dealing with the developing motor skills of children. The training of pre-
service early childhood teachers in pupil motor and
sensory skill development is a basic component in many
of the early childhood education certification programs
emerging throughout the country.

Inherent also, in such programs, is the heightened
attention being paid to the identification of perceptual and motor underachievers. Early referrals to
specialists of motor difficulties may not only help to
improve the physical outputs, mimicry, and modeling
abilities of the child, but also help alleviate the
negative effect which can result in the affective domain. For instance, Cratty, et al., report that
responses on a test of self concept from a
group of 133 children with motor problems matched to a
group of children without motor problems revealed that
the students with motor problems had a significantly more
poor self concept.[2]

Sensory deprivation as a frequent source of problems is also well documented. For instance, in experi-
ments restricting tactile, visual, and auditory stimu-
lations, adults experience hallucinations and unreason-
able fears after eight hours of confinement.[3] This

type of experiment has served to substantiate other psychological research, indicating that sensory restriction leads to disordered cognitive functioning.[4]

It becomes apparent then, that in the early childhood years the attention paid to perceptual and motor skill development is well founded. If not documented, there is, at least, an intuitive agreement that warmth and affection (the affective component) coupled with perceptual and motor development (the psychomotor component) assist and are essential requisites needed for maximum cognitive--thus "total"--development.

In spite of the growing number of preschool teacher training programs and governmental stirrings to assist them,[5] there is a growing concern about them and early education in general. For instance, Moore and Moore present a strong case that academically oriented preschooling can inhibit proper emotional growth and physical development. They conclude that long-term studies favor the later school entrant when compared to the early school entrant in total development.[6]

The Beginning Student, Psychomotor Perceiving and Activating Skills

The typical pupil enters school at age four to six. At this time, the teacher anticipates that most basic perceptive and motor skills will have reached a given level. If they have not, certain problems may be deemed severe enough so that referrals are made to specialists. These problems often fall into three categories: (1) perceptual problems, (2) gross motor difficulties, and (3) speech difficulties.

Although it is beyond the scope of this book to examine each of these in depth, a brief description of certain of these problems follows.

Specific Language Disability

The medical profession describes Specific Language Disability (SLD) as a problem encountered by 7 to 8 per cent of boys and 1 to 3 per cent of girls with average or better intelligence. These children have specific difficulty in learning to read and spell. Some of their characteristics include:

1. Poor visual perception and memory for words

   In spite of normal vision, even after repeated effort, they cannot remember the words they have studied. Recognition is either absent or poor.

2. Poor auditory memory for words or for individual sounds in words

   In spite of normal hearing, short auditory span may show up in speech or spelling, or both. Many cannot distinguish between close gradations of sound.

3. Reversal and confusion in direction

   Right and left confusion may produce reversals of words, syllables, or letters in reading, writing, or speech. Examples are: "was" for "saw," "sowro" for "sorrow," "b" for "d," "p" for "q." [Hermann labels the confusion between letters "rotations" ("b" for "d"), and the reversed sequence of letters and syllables "reversals" ("was" for "saw").] Not only may the confusion produce reversals, but also such reversals are usually more numerous and persist much longer than in other persons--far beyond what is considered to be normal learning time.

   Up and down confusion may produce inversion of letters, such as "m" for "w," or "p" for "d."

   Several other possibilities are oral mix-up of whole sentences, mirror writing of sentences, or transposition of numbers.

4. Poor recall for reproduction of simple figures

   On being shown a picture of a simple figure such as the following ——□, there may be inability to recall and

reproduce this with any degree of
accuracy--after removal of the picture. [Series of pictures is used.]

5. Ambidexterity

    Uncertainty as to which hand is more
    comfortable to use may continue--a
    slowness in establishing habitual
    right- or left-handedness. Or the use
    of the _same_ hand for the _same_ _task_ may
    be _inconsistent_.

6. Clumsiness, poor coordination

    Early clumsiness in learning any gross
    physical act may be present, and co-
    ordination required for achieving
    finer motor skills, such as game
    skills, may show up later on as below
    average. They may, however, perform
    well in large-muscle sports, such as
    swimming and football.

7. Poor ability to reproduce rhythm se-
    quences

    Reproducing short rhythm patterns by
    tapping may be difficult.

8. Speech disorders

    Stuttering, lisping, or lack of oral
    facility with language may be present,
    or speech development may have been
    slow.[7]

There does not seem to be agreement as to the
specific reason for these physiofunctional difficulties. However, there is agreement that special methods
(or therapy) are required.[8]

As has been stated in prior chapters, the prin-
cipal function of the teacher is not to correct such
disorders, but to be alert to such problems so that
proper referrals can be made.

DELIBERATE MODELING

The Principle of
Ideomotor Training

The chief strategy utilized by teachers at the
Activating level is the demonstration. Whether the
skill being demonstrated is on a film loop, modeled by
the teacher, viewed on TV, or demonstrated by fellow
students while the teacher critiques, the basic task is
to present physical skills for the student to imitate.

Because the process is so direct, it is likely
that no alternative process can improve upon it. Yet
the demonstration itself can be examined to make it
better, and empirical studies suggest ways that can
help to optimize learning rates.

In most instances, motor skill instruction follows
a predictable pattern when a demonstration is employed.
First, there is an attempt to arouse motivation ex-
trinsically, or capitalize on intrinsic desire. In
short, the teacher establishes set. Second, the
instructor engages in the behavior to be modeled, accompanied by explanation. During this modeling the
teacher may ask questions of students, students may
raise questions, or both may occur. Occasionally all
questions are deferred until the demonstration is completed. Third, the students are arranged so as to be
able to practice the skill. Fourth, the instructor
(when possible) provides feedback to individual students regarding their progress.

With this description in mind, what empirical
evidence may shed light on the process to expedite
learning? Stated succinctly, there is ample empirical
evidence to support the notion that in specific motor
task development, combining motor practice with cognitive practice is superior to the use of either cognitive practice or motor practice alone.[9]

Practice research indicates that during modeling
the timing of cognitive practice is a major factor.
During the initial acquisition of motor skills, cognitive practice is as important as motor practice.
Only in the final phases do motor skill attributes
(such as speed of movement and time of reaction) become
more important contributory factors.[10] Separate

172

research indicates that mentally rehearsing movements can improve the performance of skilled athletes about as well as motor practice.[11] Thus, a principle called "ideomotor training" emerges which implies that when teachers are attempting to work at sublevel 2.3--Deliberate Modeling, their students will learn to perform given motor tasks more quickly if allowed time for deliberate cognitive practice.

Upon reflection, it becomes clear that even though this idea seems fundamental, it is often ignored. For instance, how much time is devoted by seventh grade basketball coaches to mental practice of motor skills? How much time is devoted in typing classes to mental practice of finger dexterity? The answer is perhaps far less than the emphasis on equivalent practice of the specific physical skills desired.

In the demonstration lesson described above, mental focus occurs during all four of the steps, but traditionally there is not a period provided for mental practice. That is, a period of time is not provided in which students cognitively practice the motor skill under development.

To further illustrate the principle of ideomotor training, the following specific situation is described. Assume a teacher wishes to teach a beginning metals class the procedure to use to taper a bar on a metal lathe. Using the steps described above, a session is conducted following the demonstration in which students are asked to go over in their minds the physical movements necessary in accomplishing the task. Students are asked to practice in their minds the placing of the material in the chuck, tightening it, selecting and mounting the tool bit, adjusting machine settings, and so on. This period can be conducted both orally and/or in writing. Only after it is obvious that the student can imagine and relate these steps is he allowed to proceed to the actual motor skill practice session. In light of the research, only as the skill moves toward the Execution level is the emphasis shifted almost solely to motor practice sessions.

EXECUTING

By and large, the major portion of the task in public schools within the psychomotor domain has been

173

to move students from the Activating of physical skills through Execution of those skills. This is accomplished through opportunity to practice skills in a variety of situations. Assuming that the physical development of the student allows it, the skill level within Execution is deemed attained if its execution becomes automated, with a minimum of errors.

The strategies utilized by teachers to accomplish this end vary much more than those used at the Activating level. By far the easiest to evaluate are in the area of athletic coaching. Leaving aside the accompanying cognitive and affective components necessary to produce winning teams, why is it that some coaches seem to consistently produce team members with superior executory skills? At the professional and college level it can be attributed to the skill of staff in Performance Judging. That is, the recruiters are experts in evaluating the psychomotor ability of prospective players.

But at the public school level the reasons for the superior Executing ability of some coaches' players are not readily apparent. Certainly there are such things as a "winning syndrome" in which a winning high school team is the inspiration for upcoming youngsters to practice more often and harder. However, many coaches take their winning records with them. The answer must be, in part, attributed to superior practice schedules and procedures, but crucial also is specifying the specific outcomes (objectives).

For instance, George Allen, in his book Complete Book of Winning Football Drills, spends almost thirty pages on organizing a practice schedule, and each drill in the book includes its purpose (objective) in italics. A typical example is "The purpose of this drill is to improve close line tackling stressing head up, back firm, tail low, and feet spaced shoulder width apart for proper balance."[12]

Learning Principles and Execution

The Revelation of Objectives

There have been many studies designed to determine the effect of revealing to the learner at the outset of

174

instruction exactly what it is that he will be expected
to do. A high percentage of these studies indicate
that when the learner understands exactly what his
objective is, he learns more rapidly.[13] Thus the
teacher engaged in the teaching of psychomotor skills
should not initiate practice periods without revealing
the learning objective for those periods.

The Principle of
Perceived Purpose

The educational principle of involving students in
understanding reasons for learning and practicing
skills has been accepted by educators for some time.
Whether for all learning[14] or for specific psychomotor
skills,[15] there is agreement that learners will increase their acquisition and retention if they understand clearly the purpose for learning.

This principle is particularly important when a
complicated executory skill is broken into smaller
skills for practice purposes. The whole may be more
easily conceptualized and rationalized than a subcom-
ponent. Thus a student may be willing to learn to
execute a skill because he grasps its relation to an
overall effort, but without such a relationship the
skill may seem pointless.

In terms of strategies, the student should understand at the beginning of the practice period exactly
what he is expected to be able to do and why he needs
to be able to do it.

The Principle of
Knowledge of Results

The logic of accurate knowledge of results to
learners during practice periods cannot be ignored.
How else can active adjustments be made for improvement? Presently, instead of questioning whether or not
knowledge of results is important, more studies are
being undertaken to determine the effects of such
things as delayed feedback, verbal scores, and accu-
mulated results feedback on learning and retention.[16]
The style and immediacy of feedback to learners engaged
in skill execution improvement has become the question.
Provision for feedback is accepted as a vital part of

the psychomotor executory learning.

When planning strategies for learning and practice periods, teachers need to question whether adequate provision for feedback is provided and how it can be improved. For instance, is videotaping equipment available so that students may see their own errors? How can students provide feedback to other students? What feedback devices are uniquely available to the content area (e.g., coaching assistants, mirrors, and so on)?

The Principle of Individualizing Instruction

Because the level of development of a particular psychomotor skill is often easier to determine than the development of many cognitive or affective learnings, instruction in physical skills <u>tends</u> toward individualization. Within the psychomotor domain, the two basic procedures for achieving individualization become obvious. (1) When specific objectives have been formulated in skill areas it soon becomes apparent if prerequisite objectives are necessary for specific students. For instance, there is little sense in handing out difficult music to a beginning student if his skill level is not sufficiently advanced. (2) Teachers may find that an objective is attainable without breaking it down into prerequisite objectives, but for some students faster or more efficient learning may be attained by varying the type of learning activity in which each student engages.

These principles are not new, but each suggests a procedure that can be helpful as the teacher designs his teaching strategies.

MANEUVERING

Because instructors so often feel that there is an absolute "right way" to accomplish given ends, students are sometimes not allowed to operate at the Maneuvering level. The essence of Maneuvering is to allow the student to engage in physical operations with possible choices of skill selection. Assuming that the student can Execute basic skills, the unique task and his personal abilities will blend to create a "best" procedure for him. When possible alternate ways to accomplish the end are restricted, the student is consequently unable to compare results by identifying similarities and differences in process and results. Instead of being able to "Maneuver," he must simply "Execute."

For instance, given a particular blueprint for a machine part with tolerances in the 1/16" range, it is feasible that choices between several machines could be made. A mill, handsaw, or shaper could all possibly be used. Without an opportunity to Maneuver, the student will be restricted to Execution only on previously designated machines.

Encouraging students to operate at the Maneuvering level is necessarily a function of the teacher. The textbooks accompanying skill classes, even though they may be comprehensive, lead the teacher to view his task as primarily that of student achievement at the Execution level. As an example, Ludwig and McCarthy's Metalwork Technology and Practice is over six hundred pages long and includes a comprehensive treatment of the uses of hand tools, abrasives, grinding wheels, power sawing, drill-press operations, quality control and inspection, heat treatment, hardness testing, and numerical control machining.[17] Choices between alternative procedures are left to teacher and student.

What is meant by the often-heard expression, "He has all the skills, and with more experience can become a top ball player"? By skills the speaker is referring to psychomotor skill Execution. By "more experience" the speaker really means that with more opportunities for Maneuvering, the individual will identify the analogous relationships between on-the-spot situations to previous situations and select the best set of skills to use in given circumstances. The sports world is filled with instances where, even with mediocre executory skills, the seasoned athlete wins because of proper skill selection.

In addition to the simple process of allowing students to independently choose the skills that they wish and build maneuverability through a trial-and-error process, there are specific strategies teachers can use to speed up the process. One such technique is the use of videotaping and feedback. Seeing oneself in a physical act is superior to verbal feedback from another person. Supplemented by teacher-student planning which focuses upon success possibilities prior to actual execution, the payoff is even further enhanced.

PSYCHOMOTOR JUDGING

Depending upon the sophistication of the process of criteria formulation, psychomotor judgments can vary from the armchair quarterback's remark, "That pass was terrible!," to eight judges being within one-tenth of a point in their rating of a gymnastic performance.

The tasks of the teacher are to (1) assist students in Establishing the Performance Criteria for judging performance, (2) provide opportunities and feedback to enhance the application of a given criterion in specific circumstances so that deviation from the criterion can be accurately judged, and (3) assist students in understanding the way the process works while it is going on so that judgments will not be based on weak, limited, or inappropriate criteria.

At this level the cognitive component is obviously dominant. There is a definite difference between judging a performance skill and judging the efficiency of ideas or a conflict in values. But often the judgment is rendered with elements of all three domains.

For instance, in judging a piece of pottery, the evaluator may take into account his aesthetic responses to the pottery (affective domain), as well as the skill exhibited in the technique used (psychomotor domain). The process of building criteria and making judgments is the same. What is being judged differentiates the categories.

PSYCHOMOTOR CREATING

6.1--Combining Skills and Its Relationship to 5.2 Performance Judging

Situations within schools for practicing the Combining of Skills are plentiful. Teachers need only to be reminded of the range of possibilities that present themselves in a wide variety of areas.

To illustrate, below are several seed ideas common to various content areas:

Agriculture--Design and construction of a truck-mounted tool kit;

Art--Unique pottery shape construction;

Biological Science--New grafting tools construction;

Business--Display cases and display assembly;

Geology--Development of special equipment for rock hunts;

Geography--Designs of maps of hypothetical ideal countries;

Dance--Development of original routines;

Physical Education--Design and participation in health exercise schedules;

History--Construction of a model depicting an historical setting or event;

Home Economics--Development and production of unique recipes and menus;

Industrial Technology--Designing and building an item of furniture;

Library Science--Setting up a check-out system for books in an old folks' home;

Music--Writing and singing or playing a ballad or an instrument;

Theatre--Developing a pantomime.

At this level the student is also modifying his conceptual models and criteria by which he judges psychomotor skills. The basic strategy available to teachers to assist in this cyclical development contains two elements. First, the teacher must formally provide ideal models whenever possible. Second, when superior performance is encountered in the classroom

179

or laboratory, it must be pointed out so that the feedback encourages the acquisition of proper criteria.

During formal sessions at formulating criteria for judging, discussion of the subskills that make up the entire skill should be examined, and their relationship to the whole analyzed. When the teacher begins to involve students in trial performance judgments and encourages them to compare their ratings with those of experts, equivalent practice at the Performance Judging level has been engaged in. Thus, the judgments used when combining skills in new ways at the 6.1--Combining Skills level has reinforced and supplemented continued development at the 5.1--Establishing Performance Criteria and 4.2--Performance Judging levels.

6.2--Performance Insight

There also exist opportunities for teachers to allow for the possibility of moments of 6.2--Performance Insight by structuring environments that are compatible to it. In the thought process about performance skills, the strategies employed may contain the same elements as described for level 6 in the cognitive domain (Chapter Five). But what of the potential for creativity in direct psychomotor skills?

The problem has been succinctly put by Brown and Gaynor. "Unfortunately, creativity has had only passing interest for many physical educators. Although a number of leaders in the physical education profession since 1930 have expressed an interest in this complex and little understood force, to date there seems to have been no attempt to define carefully, within a comprehensive conceptualization, the role of creativity in physical education."[18] Brown and Gaynor go on to suggest a theoretical base and perhaps unintentionally expose a tremendous potential for research.

The process of allowing creativity to direct psychomotor activity may find a place in the dance, sculpture, or a host of other human endeavors, but it is exhibited most often in the performances in athletic contests. At times, the athlete may rise to performance heights that approach levels of accomplishment beyond the reach of ordinary humans. These instances are extraordinary and seem almost inexplicable with our present knowledge.

ENDNOTES

[1] Clare Cherry, Creative Movement for the Developing Child, A Nursery School Handbook for Non-Musicians
(Belmont California: Fearon Publishers, Inc., 1971),
pp. 13-15.

[2] Bryant J. Cratty, et al., Movement Activities,
Motor Ability, and the Education of Children (Springfield, Illinois: Charles C. Thomas, Publisher, 1970),
pp. 38-39.

[3] S. J. Friedman, H. V. Grunebaum, and M. Greenblatt,
"Perceptual and Cognitive Changes in Sensory Deprivation," in Sensory Deprivation, eds. P. Soloman, et al.
(Cambridge, Massachusetts: Harvard University Press,
1961).

[4] D. O. Hebb, The Organization of Behavior: A
Neuropsychological Theory (New York: John Wiley and
Sons, Inc., 1949).

[5] See the Child and Family Act of 1975, introduced
by Senator Walter Mondale and Representative John
Brademos, designed to support day care and early childhood education.

[6] Raymond S. Moore and Dorothy N. Moore, Better
Late Than Early: A New Approach to Your Child's Education (New York: E. P. Dutton and Company, 1975).

[7] Marion F. Stuart, Neurophysiological Insight Into
Teaching (Palo Alto, California: Pacific Books, Publishers, 1963), pp. 9-11.

[8] See, for instance, John Money, Reading Disability:
Progress and Research Needs in Dyslexia (Baltimore:
Johns Hopkins University Press, 1962).

[9] V. Eberhard, "Transfer of Training Related to
Finger Dexterity," Percept Motor Skills, 17 (1963):274; G.
Egstrom, "The Effects of an Emphasis on Conceptualizing
Techniques Upon the Early Learning of a Gross Motor

181

Skill" (Ph.D. dissertation, Department of Physical Education, University of Southern California at Los Angeles, 1961); and R. J. Stebbins, "Relationships Between the Perception and Reproduction of Certain Motor Skills," Research Quarterly, 39 (1968):3.

[10]E. A. Fleishman and W. E. Hempel, Jr., "Factoral Analysis of Complex Psychomotor Performance and Related Skills," Journal of Applied Psychology, 40 (1956):2; and E. A. Fleishman and S. Rich, "Role of Kinesthetic and Spatial-Visual Abilities in Perceptional-Motor Learning," Journal of Experimental Psychology, 66 (1963):6-11.

[11]M. Vanek and B. J. Cratty, Psychology and the Superior Athlete (New York: The Macmillan Company, 1970).

[12]George H. Allen, Complete Book of Winning Football Drills (Englewood Cliffs, New Jersey: Prentice-Hall, Inc., 1959).

[13]See Robert Kibler, et al., Objectives for Instruction (Boston: Allyn and Bacon, Inc., 1974).

[14]James Popham and Eva Baker, Systematic Instruction (Englewood Cliffs, New Jersey: Prentice-Hall, Inc., 1970), pp. 80-82.

[15]George D. Small, "The Learning Process As Applied to Coaching," Athletic Journal, 36 (1956):28-42.

[16]D. H. Holding, "Knowledge of Results," in Skills, ed. David Legge (Middlesex, England: Penguin Books Ltd., 1970), pp. 249-65.

[17]Oswald Ludwig and Willard J. McCarthy, Metalwork Technology and Practice (Bloomington, Illinois: McKnight and McKnight, 1969).

[18]George I. Brown and Donald Gaynor, "Athletic Action as Creativity," The Journal of Creative Behavior, 1 (Spring 1967):155.

CHAPTER VIII--Viewing the Three Domains

One of the major purposes of this book is
to present a classification scheme for educational objectives that will allow the practicing teacher to
utilize the analogous relationships between the three
domains as a learning tool. To this end, a three-
dimensional model is diagrammed in Figure 9. The model
is designed to assist teachers in building the mental
concepts and relationships necessary for effective
utilization of classified objectives.

THE DOMAIN CAP

The first letters of the Cognitive,
Affective, and Psychomotor Domains form a convenient
acronym (CAP) that can be organized into a model to
visually represent the relationships between the domains. Since each of the three domains is constantly
interacting with the other two, any conceptual model
formed must reflect this condition. The implication is
that the cognitive domain is influenced by, and is
influencing, both the affective and psychomotor domains.
In turn, the affective and psychomotor domains are influencing each other. Thus the model implies two considerations: (1) the domains are constantly influencing
one another, and (2) at any given level, analogous relationships exist between the three domains in the way
a level is defined and functions.

Since the degree of cognitive effort has
been used as the basic sorting factor to define levels,
an attempt has been made to indicate this in the model.
For instance, at the Judging and Creating levels,

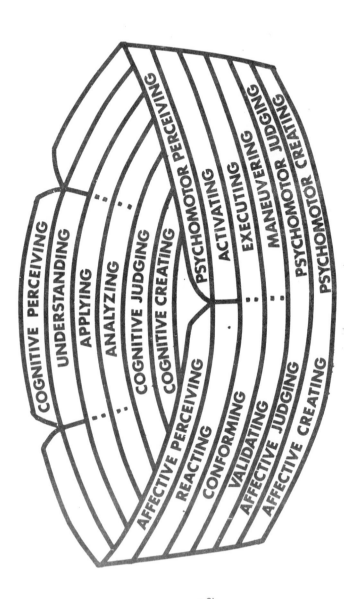

The Domain CAP
(Cognitive-Affective-Psychomotor)

Figure 9

184

cognition is so important to the affective and psychomotor domains that there are no definite lines drawn
between domains. Whether the individual is making affective judgments, cognitive judgments, or psychomotor
judgments, the operation is basically cognitive. What
is being judged determines the domain.

As the degree of cognition decreases throughout
the affective and psychomotor domains, the distinctions
between the domains at each level become increasingly
more obvious. By the time the Understanding, Reacting,
and Activating levels are reached, cognition has a
minimal influence on the other two domains.

By placing the Judging and Creating levels closest
to the brain when the CAP is worn, the observer is reminded that these are the highest cognitive levels.
By increasing the severity or distinctness of the lines
between domains as the move toward less cognition is
made, the reader is reminded of the decreasing amount
of cognition used at each level.

RELATIONSHIPS BETWEEN THE DOMAINS

In many types of learning, the mind can grasp the
essence of a new set of concepts if there are analogous
relationships to a familiar area. Once the cognitive
classification scheme has been mastered, the affective
and psychomotor domain schemes are easier to understand
because of the parallels to the cognitive domain. In
fact, the analogies can be rather startling.

LEVEL 1:   COGNITIVE PERCEIVING-
AFFECTIVE PERCEIVING-
PSYCHOMOTOR PERCEIVING

At the lowest level, the unique function of each
domain is most distinct. Each domain functions in
specific ways that are similar to the others, but not
as closely related as at the higher levels. The
psychomotor domain provides the sensory channels to
relay inputs to the brain. The brain perceives meaning
by focusing, and builds emotive sets by imprinting the
transmission. The body and brain then store those
inputs for physical, mental, or emotive responses.

185

LEVEL 2: UNDERSTANDING-
REACTING-ACTIVATING

At the next level, the outputs begin to take on analogous relationships. The brain retrieves data from the cognitive bank, but the affective imprint that colors outputs when a specific stimulus is presented also affects the output style. This result is displayed to the observer in the form of physical behavior.

As more cognition is utilized by the individual, he begins to manipulate the data for better understanding and conceptualizing. In a sense, to "control" it. The data may be changed from one form to another.

In the affective domain, the individual is attempting to gain control over emotional reactions resulting from severe imprints. The individual seeks to change the output from one form to another (perhaps unacceptable behavior to acceptable behavior).

In the physical domain, the polishing of physical outputs develops. An attempt to control the body has begun. The individual begins to model the physical movements of others; i.e., to change his movements from one form to another.

LEVEL 3: APPLYING-
CONFORMING-EXECUTING

At the next level, the essence of the analogous relationship between the three domains can be depicted by the word "Useability." This is the level at which most people operate a high percentage of the time.

In the cognitive domain, the individual is using rules and principles (albeit sometimes complex) to obtain answers. In the affective domain, he is using handy, conventional, or socially acceptable rationales for attitudes adopted, and in the psychomotor domain, the individual is using developed motor skills to accomplish arrays of physical tasks.

LEVEL 4: ANALYZING-
VALIDATING-MANEUVERING

At this level, in all three domains the individual
has begun to deal with problems having a "right" answer
available, and by comparing and contrasting the problem
with similar problems previously encountered, is able
to determine the solution.

In the cognitive domain, ideas and concepts are
comparatively and logically analyzed for solutions.
In the affective domain, values are similarly examined
and accepted, and in the psychomotor domain, physical
skills are inspected and appropriate ones selected for
motor needs.

LEVEL 5: COGNITIVE-AFFECTIVE-
PSYCHOMOTOR JUDGING

By the time an individual reaches this level, the
actual operation has become highly cognitive. The relationship is so strikingly similar that it is beyond
analogy, and really is the same function but with different content and results.

In all three domains, the individual establishes
criteria to make a judgment, and then renders the
judgment. In the affective domain, however, there are
emotional overtones that have a subtle influence on
the decision-making process. In the psychomotor domain, there are kinesthetic reactions that influence
such evaluations. In the "pure" cognitive domain,
ideas may be theoretically judged with objectivity.

LEVEL 6: COGNITIVE-AFFECTIVE-
PSYCHOMOTOR CREATING

At the highest level in the three domains, the
operation is the same, with only the content changed.
An environment is created in which an insightful
moment of creativity may occur, and on occasion, this
phenomenon takes place. It may be an inspiration about
values, a creative insight about ideas, or a unique notion about a motor performance.

The reader has now been afforded an opportunity to review the most obvious analogous relationships between the three domains. Space prohibits an in-depth examination of all possible analogous relationships. However, as the reader engages in thought about the domains and their levels, he may well be intrigued by the discovery of new relationships.

ACHIEVING DOMAIN BALANCE

STRUGGLES FOR
DOMAIN DOMINANCE

Some of the most striking illustrations of the need to maintain domain balance exist in the world of sports. The three domains are easily identified and proper balance is essential for victory. In competitive sports, the individual or team needs (1) proper execution (psychomotor), (2) motivation and poise (affective), and (3) game strategy (cognitive). With any of these three lacking, a team or individual in competition will appear inept.

The most obvious element to note in a sports event is the lack of proper execution. Mistakes such as the dropped pass or football fumble, the missed right hook in a boxing match, or the missed free throw in basketball are readily observed by the fan. More subtle errors, such as the failure to execute a line block in football, or failure to properly screen a man in basketball, are spotted by the players and coaches. Deficiencies in the other two domains are more difficult to detect. On occasion, a team that has poor executory skills will beat a team with superior skills. When this happens, the fault may be in motivation and poise, in poor game plans, or both. A domain balance was not maintained by the losing team.

Many of the common clichés and phrases used by coaches and sports writers are efforts to identify the domain in which a deficiency existed that caused a win or loss. Some samples follow, along with the domain to which the speaker (probably unconsciously) refers.

Psychomotor Clichés

1. "They have a better recruiting program" (able to procure ballplayers with superior skills).

2. "Their team strength is awesome."

3. "He (the opponent's coach) just has the horses to work with."

4. "They blew us out of the gym" (the opponent's physical ability was so much better that game plans and motivation could not compensate).

Affective Clichés

1. "We were just down."

2. "That blocked punt broke our back" (spirit).

3. "Practices were listless all week."

4. "They just were not to be denied today."

5. "They were overconfident."

Cognitive Clichés

1. "Their trick plays killed us."

2. "Our players weren't prepared for a zone defense."

3. "We went into a stall too early."

4. "We should have had Jones run the mile instead of the two mile."

All of these are common statements which allude to a domain that is being held responsible for a loss or low score. A few coaches also will say "We just made too many mistakes," leaving the listener to guess the domain.

In most endeavors in which people engage, the psychomotor area is a bystander. If, however, a public official bumps his head, stumbles, or makes other psychomotor "goofs," the press will point such errors out. The interplay between the cognitive and affective domains involves people in a constant struggle. Rightly or wrongly, society has chosen to vary its reinforcement from domain to domain; sometimes affective dominance is encouraged, while at other times cognitive dominance is expected. At a ballet performance, film, church, or political rally, people want to see and listen to people who are emotionally "keyed up" and who will, in turn, excite them. In most other endeavors, however, people are expected to behave like Perry Mason--with cognitive efficiency. If an individual allows one domain or the other to dominate most of the time, he may be labeled with terms such as "cold turkey" or "pollyanna."

The balance that is expected between the affective and cognitive domains will also vary from society to society. For instance, there seems to be more reward for the German or Japanese who can control his emotions, while Mexicans and Italians feel comfortable in a much more emotionally demonstrative setting.

SHIFTS IN DOMAIN EMPHASIS

In American society, the "ideal" business person is describable in terms of the domains. He is intelligent and uses the full range of cognitive abilities well, especially the ultimate levels at which he renders judgmental decisions that could make or break the firm or has creative insights that will increase production or sales. He is allowed the affective attributes that society considers acceptable, such as empathy for employees, contentiousness, good humor, ambition, and tolerance. His values have been thought out enough so that affective behavior patterns are consistent, and in value conflicts, judgments are based on a value hierarchy that seems appropriate to fellow workers and superiors. Physical movements are smooth, and accomplished with minimum effort. He either jogs each morning, plays tennis and golf at the club, or handball at the Y. When asked to render opinions regarding major sports events or sports figures, he can make judgments based upon explainable criteria that seem reasonable to business associates and friends.

Other occupational or professional groups tend to favor a "balance" that places more emphasis on one

190

domain than another. The journeyman working for someone else operates (and usually wants to operate) no
higher than the application level cognitively. He
understands all the necessary principles and procedures and can apply them when given a particular task.
He may well take pride, however, in certain psychomotor
abilities. There is no doubt about his executing
ability, and he manipulates well to expedite work. The
worker may be proud of a unique psychomotor approach
formulated to accomplish a given type of job, and
renders judgments about the performance skills of fellow workers with consummate skill.

In the stereotype of many such occupational groups,
the affective domain is viewed as being primarily
operational at the Conforming level. The Walter
Cranstons and Archie Bunkers are amusing because they
have not validated their values or settled on value
hierarchies, and therefore trip over themselves with
inconsistencies.

In some professions, the interplay of the domains
settles on cognitive and psychomotor skills. This is
especially true of the surgeon who also is involved
in diagnostic and procedural judgments. In some
clinics with repetitive operations, some surgeons become performance dominated. For instance, they repeat
a hip replacement over and over without other involvement. They have developed a particular executing
skill and are hired to perform that skill.

In other occupational areas, differences exist between jobs because of differing cognitive level requirements. Often when the shift to a higher cognitive
level occurs, a concomitant recognition of prestige
and salary increase accompanies it. An example exists
in job levels connected with clerk, bookkeeper, accountant, and C.P.A. The clerk will operate at the
applying level with a handful of rules and procedures
to follow. The bookkeeper's set of rules is much more
involved. The accountant is responsible for a degree
of analysis and occasional judgments, and the C.P.A.
must render many crucial judgments (for instance,
which accounting procedure is judged best for particular tax purposes). As each job moves to higher levels
in the cognitive domain, the responsibilities and
monetary rewards increase.

Similarly, in a job shop (i.e., metal refinishing,
or tool-and-die shop) the roles are ranked by cognition.

The punch press operator is paid less than the tool-and-die maker because the task performed does not rise above the application and execution levels. The tool-and-die maker must be able to read blueprints and then make decisions as to the best procedure to follow when assembling dies (manipulation). The foreman is paid still more because he must render judgments as to the best way to expedite the work through the plant. The tool-and-die engineer receives the top dollar, however, because he must arrange procedures to accomplish given tasks and make crucial judgments as to the appropriate bids for jobs that will obtain work for the plant, and still make a profit. Perhaps he may achieve a performance or creative insight leading to a profit breakthrough.

There are a few endeavors, however, in which man has artificially created a situation in which the three domains are equally valid and crucial and are made vivid because the fear of death amplifies and glorifies the setting. This is true to some extent in auto racing, but it finds its full potential in the bullfight. In reviewing a great bullfight, a writer could dwell on each of the domains with equal emphasis. In the cognitive domain, the matador must judge the strengths and weaknesses of the bull in order to maximize the potential of his passes. He must give instructions to the picadors and banderillos to correct, through proper placement of their instruments, tendencies for the bull to move to the left or right, hook, or stop. And he must make the ultimate judgment of how much risk to take to extract a full performance.

Affectively, the matador must control his own emotions so that the excitement of the moment does not carry him to the point of taking more risk than is justifiable or become so fearful he errs. He must have firm command of his value hierarchy and understand the value hierarchy of the crowd. Equally important, each bullfight presents an ultimate value conflict. The matador's success and prestige depend upon his ability to please the crowd. But the crowd is most pleased when risks are being taken. So the matador must resolve the conflict between the value of his own life and the value of living that life with honor, prestige, and wealth.

The ultimate moment in the bullfight happens rarely, but when it does, the spectator is lifted to

such ecstacy that he will return time and again in the
hope that it will be repeated. This is the moment in
which the matador can insightfully create (cognitive-,
affective-, and performance-wise) a moment of artistry
like few other possible experiences.

DOMAIN EMPHASIS
IN THE SCHOOLS

Currently, the most direct, albeit oversimplified,
statement that can be made about domain balance in the
schools is that there is a predominant emphasis on the
cognitive; there are a few instances of psychomotor-
oriented classes; and work in the affective domain is
usually left to chance.

This state of affairs is in need of remediation.
In a school with domain balance, each domain would have
its rightful place in the curriculum. Although a complete description of such a school is deserving of a
volume unto itself, a brief outline of the possible
structure for such a secondary school follows.

THE GOAL-ORIENTED, DOMAIN-
BALANCED SECONDARY SCHOOL

Upon entering Capland Heights Secondary School,
each youngster undergoes a comprehensive assessment
process. In the cognitive domain, a set of instruments
is administered that identifies deficiencies according
to Guilford's Structure of Intellect model.[1] This
classification scheme for a multitude of aspects of
human intelligence allows for a comprehensive identification of areas of needed remediation. (Up to 120
separate ability measures are theoretically possible.)

In the affective domain, the Kohlberg classification system for moral development[2] is used to identify
the level of moral development of each student. In
addition, personality tests will be administered to
identify inadequacies in self concept and/or dominant
emotional traits.

In the psychomotor domain, each student receives a
complete physical. Subsequently, complete batteries of
physical skill tests will be administered that will

measure sensory input, endurance, and dexterity.

The sum of this data will be submitted to a
trained diagnostician. If necessary, this expert may
seek the help of specialists in each domain. From the
diagnosis, an educational plan is designed for each
individual to bring him to a minimum competency level
in each domain.

For the cognitive domain, a huge inventory of
self-instructional packages comprehensively covering
all the cells in Guilford's Structure of Intellect are
available. These are woven into subject-matter content
areas appropriate for each grade level. A portion of
each day is available for individual work in a self-
paced structure, with advisors on call to assist with
problems and to help motivate and organize work plans.
Additionally, the plan described for the student may
call for small and/or large group subject-matter
classes. In this instance, the instructor is informed
of the specific areas in which the student needs help,
and the teacher tailors assignments and questions to
focus on these areas. All of this effort is continually monitored to ensure a balance throughout the
levels of the cognitive domain.

In the affective domain, all students spend time
in a small group led by a counselor-psychologist who
has been trained in the Kohlberg theory and the Pierce-
Gray classification model. These sessions are not
sensitivity training or therapy sessions, but inquiries
into moral dilemmas. The objective is to assist the
students to (1) operate efficiently at levels 2 to 6
in the Pierce-Gray classification scheme--that is,
(2) to identify and qualify values, to integrate them,
and to use them in making value judgments, and (3) to
move up in the levels of Moral Development.

In the academic classroom, the student is given
opportunities to study the relationship of each content
area to the whole of man's knowledge. The content of
each subject area is examined in terms of its particular value to man and society so that the student can
better relate it to his own value hierarchy. There is
no indoctrination or forced "appreciation," simply
concerted assistance toward a logical and consistent
value integration.

For the student with personality problems or
psychological difficulties, individual and group therapy

is available. Since the objectives of the total educational experience are spelled out precisely, these sessions are viewed as a way to help students achieve the objectives more easily by removing personal psychological obstacles.

To complete the triad, the psychomotor domain receives its fair share of attention. First, all physical needs are met. Many educators assume that in this day and age there are few physical needs that are not fulfilled. The following statistics are worth contemplating.

High school teachers instruct approximately 150 to 200 students each day. Research-based estimates indicate that in an average group of that number:

1. Five to ten will have speech defects requiring attention if therapy has not been provided in elementary school.

2. Three to six are afflicted with hearing loss serious enough to require medical attention.

3. Twenty to fifty require corrective lenses to achieve "normal" vision.

4. Ten to fifteen suffer from known allergies, such as exzema, asthma, hay fever, and hives.

5. One to ten have epilepsy, diabetes, or cardiac disability.[3]

Assured that physically the student is functioning as well as can be expected, a comprehensive array of skill games, competitions, and endurance activities is engaged in to maintain muscle tone, stamina, and alertness. Additionally, each teacher views the psychomotor domain as an essential ingredient in balanced living. As such, when moments of psychomotor use emerge, they are attended to with care and respect. For instance, in a mathematics class, compasses are not simply distributed for use. A psychomotor demonstration lesson to ensure modeling and executing behaviors in compass use is conducted with as much care as the understanding and application lesson to discover and use the formula $A = \pi r^2$.

As with the cognitive relationship to the affective domain, students are provided with opportunities to develop their personally integrated set of values built upon exposure to the facts of man's use and needs in the psychomotor domain.

The product of such a school has received assistance in correcting deficiencies in all areas of cognition as defined by the Guilfordian Structure of Intellect model, and has been given a balanced experience at each level in the cognitive domain. He understands what a value hierarchy is and has begun to build values and their rationales in organized patterns. These assets are complemented by an aura of physical well being with a competence in psychomotor skills that have been selected with care.

THE RIGHT AND LEFT HEMISPHERES OF THE BRAIN AND THE THREE DOMAINS

There have been increasing thought and investigation given to the relationships of various parts of the brain to specific mental, affective, and physical functions. Some studies have found evidence indicating that there is a dominant use of the left side of the brain for language and symbolic thought and use of the right side for affective endeavors. Some educators have suggested that the "right side" (affective) of the brain has been educationally neglected to the benefit of the "left side" of the brain.[4]

This is an intriguing line of investigation, and bears watching. With the use of more and more sophisticated technical equipment such as the Ertl Index[5] and the electroencephalograph, it may be that "readings" can be taken that will indicate domain deficiencies or dominance. Sorting activities by "brain" monitoring may ultimately become a useful educational tool.

ENDNOTES

[1] J. P. Guilford, The Nature of Human Intelligence (New York: McGraw-Hill Book Company, Inc., 1967).

[2] Lawrence Kohlberg, "Stage and Sequence: The Cognitive Developmental Approach to Socialization," in *Handbook of Socialization Theory and Research*, ed. D. A. Goslin (Chicago: Rand McNally, 1969).

[3] Marvin Alcorn, James S. Kinder, and Jim R. Schunert, *Better Teaching in Secondary Schools* (New York: Holt, Rinehart and Winston, 1970), p. 21.

[4] Max R. Rennels, "Cerebral Symmetry: An Urgent Concern for Education," *Phi Delta Kappan*, 57 (March 1976):471-72; and Richard D. Konicek, "Seeking Synergism for Man's Two-Hemisphere Brain," *Phi Delta Kappan*, 57 (September 1975):37-39.

[5] William Tracy, "Goodby IQ, Hello EI (Ertl Index)," *Phi Delta Kappan*, 54 (October 1972):89-94.

APPENDICES

PIERCE-GRAY CLASSIFICATION MODEL FOR THE COGNITIVE, AFFECTIVE, AND PSYCHOMOTOR DOMAINS
(Deciphering the Learning Domains)

COGNITIVE DOMAIN	AFFECTIVE DOMAIN	PSYCHOMOTOR DOMAIN
1. COGNITIVE PERCEIVING 1.1 Focusing 1.2 Storing	1. AFFECTIVE PERCEIVING 1.1 Emotive Imprinting 1.2 Response Setting	1. PSYCHOMOTOR PERCEIVING 1.1 Sensory Transmission 1.2 Physiofunctional Maintenance
2. UNDERSTANDING 2.1 Retrieving 2.2 Rendering 2.3 Conceptualizing	2. REACTING 2.1 Emoting 2.2 Recognizing 2.3 Controlling	2. ACTIVATING 2.1 Physical Outputs 2.2 Mimicry 2.3 Deliberate Modeling
3. APPLYING 3.1 Routine Application 3.2 Procedural Application 3.3 Complex Application	3. CONFORMING 3.1 Artificial Attitude 3.2 Consistent Attitude 3.3 Rationalized Attitude	3. EXECUTING 3.1 Task Execution 3.2 Operational Execution 3.3 Skilled Execution
4. ANALYZING 4.1 Comparative Analysis 4.2 Logical Analysis	4. VALIDATING (Processing Values) 4.1 Examining Values 4.2 Accepting Values	4. MANEUVERING 4.1 Inspecting Skills 4.2 Selecting Skills
5. COGNITIVE JUDGING 5.1 Establishing Ideational Criteria 5.2 Ideational Judging (Criteria based decision from alternatives)	5. AFFECTIVE JUDGING 5.1 Establishing Value Criteria 5.2 Value Judging (Criteria based decision resolving value conflict)	5. PSYCHOMOTOR JUDGING 5.1 Establishing Performance Criteria 5.2 Performance Judging (Criteria based decision from alternatives)
6. COGNITIVE CREATING 6.1 Uniting Ideas 6.2 Creative Insight	6. AFFECTIVE CREATING 6.1 Integrating Values 6.2 Inspirational Insight	6. PSYCHOMOTOR CREATING 6.1 Combining Skills 6.2 Performance Insight

MODEL FOR THE ANALYSIS AND COMPARISON
OF CULTURAL VALUE SYSTEMS*
(With Probing Questions)

Model Categories	Sample Probing Questions
1. Identifying and clarifying dominant values (of culture and/or subgroups) This would include a thorough study and analysis of the culture for the purpose of determining those collectively held assumptions about and orientations toward the things that matter most. It should lead to the identification of a set of dominant value themes (perhaps not more than ten or twelve in number).	•What are the people of the culture willing to die for? •How are they oriented toward other peoples and toward the supernatural? •What are their heroes like, and how do they honor or reward respected individuals? •What kind of things do they accumulate and discard? •What do they laugh and cry about? •What kind of things do they consider beautiful? •How are they oriented toward authority, nature, and causality?
2. Determining the factors that contributed to the creation of the dominant values This would include a study of the history and geography of the culture in order to identify and illuminate value-creating experiences	•To what extent have the values of the culture changed over the years? •How can you account for the changes (or lack of change)?

Model Categories	Sample Probing Questions
and environments. The study of history should reveal which shaped the distinctive value pattern. The study of geography should make clear the impact of such things as resources, climate, and topography upon the value pattern of the culture.	•To what extent have their values been influenced or shaped by historical events, the physical environment, or contacts with other peoples? •Are there certain ideas, individuals, or events which apparently gave rise to their pattern of values?
3. Determining the means by which dominant values are transmitted from generation to generation This would include a careful study of the culture's systems and techniques of value transmission; it would consist mainly of a study of institutions and various processes of socialization and social control.	•Who is responsible for the training of children and young people in the culture? •How is it done, and what are they taught? •For what are young people punished, and how are they punished? •How can young people gain respect and rewards? •Are young people encouraged to have original ideas? •What kind of changes are most usually noted from generation to generation?
4. Determining the contemporary influences (or factors) tending to change the dominant values	•Do most of the people in the culture seem to behave in a manner consistent with their professed major values?

Model Categories	Sample Probing Questions
This would include a study of the instruments and techniques of value alteration in the culture; it would include a study of those institutions, folkways, and pressures which tend to create new values as well as those which alter or destroy traditional values. It would be hoped that students would come to understand that even though values tend to be static, a culture's value conflicts and inconsistencies and the pressures exerted by other cultures and by technological advances create change.	•Are there very many new ideas noted in the culture? •Do you note any new ideas that appear to conflict with any of the traditional ideas or values? •Is the culture threatened in any way by forces or ideas from the outside? If so, specify. •Is there very much difference between the values of the young and the values of adults? •Do young people do or believe very many things that their parents did not do or believe at the same age? Specify.
5. Formulating predictive hypotheses about patterns of behavior This would include practice in tracing the behavioral implications of value configurations in order to make predictions of possible patterns of behavior. It would be hoped that students would come to realize that a culture's behavior is usually reasonably consistent with its values; and therefore, a rough degree of prediction is possible.	•What might people in the culture find objectionable in culture B? In culture C? Why so? •What might people in the culture be likely to do if confronted with problem X? With problem Y? Why so? •If asked to select a new leader, what characteristics would the people of the culture look for in prospective leaders? Why so?

Model Categories	Sample Probing Questions
	•If given a choice between A, B, or C, which one would a person from the culture be most likely to choose? Why?
6. Analyzing the nature of value conflicts

This would include a study of the major social problems of the culture in an effort to identify the values involved. It would be hoped that students would come to realize that what a culture defines as a social problem is indicative of its value system; and that social problems are difficult to solve because they are in essence nothing more than conflicts between things that are valued. | •What are the major problems facing the culture?

•Are these recognized by the people of the culture as problems, or merely by you as an observer?

•What are the most common kinds of disagreements noted among the people of the culture?

•Are some people failing to conform to traditional ways of behavior? If so, who? Why so?

•Are some people trying to introduce new ideas and ways of behavior?

•How are they dealt with?

•In what ways does the culture seem to be changing (if at all)?

•Will such changes have any effect on traditional values? Specify. |
| 7. Comparing cultural value systems (past and present)

This would include practice in comparing different (or | •What beliefs do the two cultures have in common?

•What differences do you note? |

Model Categories	Sample Probing Questions
alternative) value systems in terms of their unique-ness and commonality with reference to: (a) dominant values, (b) origins, (c) modes of transmission, (d) stability and change, (e) predictive implica-tions, and (f) conflicts and social problems.	•How can you account for these similarities and differences? •What problems does cul-ture A have that culture B does not have? Why the difference? •Why does culture A value X and culture B reject X? •Which culture is under-going the greatest amount of change? Why do you think so? •In which of the two cul-tures would you prefer to live? Explain the rea-sons for your choice.

[#]Model categories and descriptions adapted from ideas suggested in Marion Brady, "The Key Concept," Social Education, 33 (November 1967):601; and from a related teaching model (including probing questions) appearing in Charles E. Gray, "Value Inquiry and the Social Studies," Education, 93 (November-December 1972):130-37.

HEURISTIC EVALUATIVE MODEL
(Analysis and Testing of Value Judgments)

Teaching Procedures	Sample Probing Questions
A. <u>Phenomenon</u>	
1. Introduction and general identification of the object, person, event, behavior, policy, or state of affairs to be evaluated (hereafter referred to as the <u>object</u>)	- What do you know about the object?
	- What have you heard others say about it?
a. Focus upon prior learnings related to the object	- Did you know that Mr. A had this to say about it?
b. Encourage a variety of responses reflecting both cognitive and affective frames-of-reference regarding the object	- What would Mr. B think of Mr. A's comment? Why so?
	- Do any of you approve of the object? Why so?
	- Who disagrees with that comment? Why?
c. Make available a set of inconsistent and contradictory proposals, interpretations, and implications with reference to the object	- Are we really talking about the same thing?
2. Descriptive and definitional analysis and clarification of the object	(<u>Descriptive</u>)
	- Who has actually seen the object?
a. Descriptive and contextual clarification of a singular, concrete, describable object	- What is it like?
	- Could it be described differently?

Teaching Procedures	Sample Probing Questions
1) Descriptive information (i.e., relevant observed or recorded data)	- Why the difference? - Is it sometimes confused with object B? Why?
2) Contextual information (i.e., clarification of special or unique circumstances or situational stipulations)	- Are we agreed now as to which object we are talking about? - How might the object be classified or categorized?
3) Subsumptive classification (i.e., object sumsumed as an instance of a more general object)	- What distinguishes it from other objects in this category?
b. Definitional meaning of a general, abstract, definable object (e.g., terms, concepts, ideas)	(Definitional) - Who can give an example of the object? - Are there others?
1) Denotative meanings (e.g., specific instances or examples and operational definitions)	- How about A, B, or C? - What characteristics do these examples have in common? How do they differ?
2) Connotative meanings (e.g., defining attributes and characteristics?	- Are we really interested in investigating all of the things that are sometimes classified as instances of the object?
3) Stipulated meaning (if necessary in order to proceed)	- Do we need a new term to identify what we are concerned with, perhaps an adjective modifier? Any suggestions?

Teaching Procedures	Sample Probing Questions
	– For our purposes, how might we define the object? – Does this sound helpful? Can we proceed?

B. Appraisal or Prescription
 	
3. Solicitation of student reactions to the clarified and defined object. Presentation of alternative reactions when students are in essential agreement. Reactions to be classified in the following manner:
 	
   a. Appraising reactions (e.g., approval-disapproval, ratings, like-dislike, preferential and derogatory comments, and so on)
 	
   b. Prescriptive reactions (e.g., injunctions, admonitions; mainly oughts and ought-nots)
	– Now, since we have defined (or described) the object, what are some of your reactions or feelings about it?
	
	– Do you approve, disapprove, or are you neutral?
	
	– Do you like or dislike it?
	
	– Does anyone have any strong feelings about what ought to be done (or believed) regarding such things?
	
	– How many differing viewpoints do we have?
	
	– Are there others that you have heard expressed elsewhere?
	
	– How about this quote from Mr. A?

C. Warrant (Justification) 4. Probing and questioning of students for the	– Who would like to defend position A? Position B?

Teaching Procedures	Sample Probing Questions
purpose of determining the reasons for their appraising and prescriptive reactions to the object. Reasons to be classified in the following manner:	- Why did you react as you did; what are your reasons?
a. Reasons reflecting criterial judgments: When the reasons offered indicate that the initial reaction was prompted by the acceptance of specific rules or a set of criteria	- Do you disapprove of the object because it is contrary to something else you believe? Explain your thinking.
	- Do you like the object because you believe it will bring about something else? Explain your thinking.
b. Reasons reflecting consequential judgments: When the reasons offered indicate that the initial reaction was prompted by the belief that certain consequences would be likely to follow from (or be caused by) the object	- Would you feel uncomfortable if you were asked to take a contrary point of view? Why?
	- How many different kinds of reasons have we had presented?
	- Can any of these be backed up or proved?
	- How might you justify your position, Bill?
c. Reasons reflecting preferential judgments: When the reasons offered indicate that the initial reaction was prompted by certain personal preferences or general attitudes, dispositions, and feelings which are activated when the student is confronted by the object	

Teaching Procedures	Sample Probing Questions
5. Application of procedures appropriate for testing and justifying all instances of criterial, consequential, and preferential value judgments	
a. <u>Criterial Judgments</u>: Justified on the basis of logical entailment. Such judgments are justified if it can be demonstrated that the object is consistent with or conforms to a given value, or explicit system or scheme of values (usually stated in the form of rules or criteria) accepted (and valued) by the individual or group making the judgment.	
Thus, criterial judgments are <u>formally warranted</u>, and therefore require a <u>logical test involving</u> steps such as the following:	(<u>Criterial</u>) - Are you clear about what the object is? - Are you sure that the object is consistent with A (the warrant)?
1) Precise definition or description of the object being evaluated	- Can you clarify what you mean by A?
2) Explicit statement of the value(s), rules, or criteria serving as the formal warrant for	- How might you go about proving that the object is consistent with A?

Teaching Procedures	Sample Probing Questions
the evaluation	– Are there any other factors upon which you might base your reaction to the object?
3) Determine, by means of logical inference, whether or not the object is logically implied by the warrant	
b. Consequential Judgments: Justified on the basis of instrumental utility. Such judgments are justified if it can be demonstrated that the object will produce or be followed by a particular effect or state of affairs that is valued by the individual or group making the judgment. The object has extrinsic value for the judger(s).	
Thus, consequential judgments are factually warranted, and therefore require an empirical test involving steps such as the following:	(Consequential) – Are you clear about what the object is?
1) Precise definition or description of the object being evaluated	– Are you sure the object will lead to A (the warrant)? – Can you clarify what you mean by A?
2) Precise definition or description of the valued effect or state of affairs	– How might you go about proving the relationship?

214

Teaching Procedures	Sample Probing Questions
serving as the contingent factual warrant for the evaluation	- Are there any other factors upon which you might base your reaction to the object?
3) Determine, by means of experimental observation or historical verification, whether or not the object is likely to produce or be followed by the valued consequence	
c. Preferential Judgments: Justified on the basis of affective worth for the individual or group making the judgment. Such judgments are justified if it can be demonstrated that the object is consistent with and in harmony with an individual's character, personality, or self concept; if it is integrally related to his philosophy of life to the extent that it is equated with "what he is" and "what he wants to be." The object has intrinsic value for the judger(s).	
Thus, preferential judgments are systemically warranted, and require a	(Preferential) - Clearly specify what you mean by the object

215

Teaching Procedures	Sample Probing Questions
subjective test (i.e., introspective self-analysis) involving steps such as the following: 1) Precise definition or description of the object being evaluated. 2) Explicit statement of a philosophy of life to which one subscribed (and a commitment to behavior consistent with the philosophy) 3) Determine, by means of introspective self-analysis and logical inference, whether or not the object is consistent with the stated philosophy of life (or with "what one is" and "what one wants to be")	- Are you sure that the object fits your life-style or philosophy of life? - Would you prefer the object over A, B, or C? - In what kind of circumstances would you reject the object and accept something else instead? - How would your life be different if you were to reject the object? - How do other people feel about the object? - Do other people accept or reject the object for reasons different from yours? - How do you feel about your positions? Why?

D. Generalized Evaluation

6. Formulation and application of generalized evaluation(s) a. Formulation of a general statement that combines the appraisal	- Can you state the complete evaluation in a more general way? - If you personally wanted to apply the basic idea of this evaluation to

216

Teaching Procedures	Sample Probing Questions
(or prescription) with the tested warrant	all times and places, how would you state it?
1) Form for generalized evaluation: "All objects warranted in this way are to be appraised (or prescribed) in this way."	- How about stating it in this general form? "All things like this are good (or bad)!"
2) Example: Phenomenon: World War I Appraisal: Bad Warrant: Loss of life (tested) Generalized Evaluation: Anything resulting in the loss of life is bad	
b. Presentation of instances of other objects that fit (conform to) the tested warrant	- Do you feel the same way about all things that are consistent with A (the warrant)? What about X?
1) Determine whether or not students are inclined to employ the same appraisal (or prescription) in all such instances	- Do you feel the same way about all things that lead to A (the warrant)? What about Z?
2) Reexamination and reassessment of reactions, reasons,	- Do you feel the same way about all things that are consistent with your life-style? What about Y?

Teaching Procedures	Sample Probing Questions
judgments, and so on (open-ended and in nonthreat environment)	- Has anyone changed his position? Why?
	- Is anyone confused? How so?
	- Do you want to evaluate the tested warrant that supports your value judgment?
	- Do you want to evaluate any of the other objects that fit your tested warrants?

Sample Evaluations

(Keyed to: Heuristic Evaluative Model diagram
Figure 4, Chapter Six)

Example #1:

A. Giving of alms to the poor

B. Good (i.e., appraised as a good act)

C. Sample statements of specific warrants: (Why is it good?)

    a. It helps fulfill the needs of the poor (consequential warrant).

    b. It makes the giver happy (consequential warrant).

    c. It is consistent with a major tenet of the Judao-Christian system of ethical behavior (rule or criterial warrant).

d. It is something I have consistently done
    throughout my adult life and I wouldn't feel
    happy with myself if I did otherwise whenever I
    encounter someone in need (preferential war-
    rant).

D. Sample generalized statements of evaluations
    (matched with a, b, c, d, above)

    a. Anything that helps fulfill the needs of the
        poor is good.

    b. Anything that makes a giver happy is good.

    c. Anything that is consistent with a major tenet
        of the Judao-Christian system of ethical be-
        havior is good.

    d. Anything that I have consistently done through-
        out my adult life and wouldn't feel happy with
        myself if I didn't do is good.

Example #2

A. Legalization of abortion

B. Ought not to be done (i.e., negative prescription)

C. Sample statements of specific warrants: (Why ought
    not to be done?)

    a. It would result in the termination of human
        life (consequential warrant).

    b. It would encourage sexual promiscuity (conse-
        quential warrant).

    c. It would be contrary to the dictates of my
        religion (criterial or rule warrant).

    d. It would upset me and make me sad to think that
        such a thing could go on around me. I wouldn't
        want to do it myself; I wouldn't want my
        friends to do it; and I wouldn't want my chil-
        dren to do it! It just goes against my grain
        (preferential warrant).

219

D. Sample generalized statements of evaluations
(<u>matched</u> <u>with</u> <u>a</u>, <u>b</u>, <u>c</u>, <u>d</u>, above)

a. Anything that would result in the termination
of human life ought not to be allowed.

b. Anything that would encourage sexual promiscu-
ity ought not to be allowed.

c. Anything that would be contrary to the dictates
of my religion ought not to be allowed.

d. Anything that I wouldn't do or want my friends
or children to do, and that upsets and makes me
sad, ought not to be allowed.

APPENDIX D

DEVELOPMENT OF MORAL JUDGMENT (OR REASONING)[*]
An Edited Compendium of the Kohlberg Theory

Charles E. Gray
Illinois State University

Soon after the turn of the twentieth century, John Dewey formulated a developmental theory of moral reasoning; Jean Piaget elaborated on the theory in the 1930s. Lawrence Kohlberg and Robert Selman of Harvard University have further refined the theory through over fifteen years of research into the way children and adults reason about moral problems (or dilemmas).

Kohlberg and Selman maintain that there are three levels of moral judgment (or reasoning); they subdivide the three levels into six major stages (two stages for each level). It is their contention that as people mature, they move step by step from stage one to stage two, to stage three, and so forth. They indicate that everyone starts at stage one early in life, but that very few people ever move beyond stage four to stage five or six. Thus, the reasoning of most adults can be classified as primarily stage three or stage four. The Kohlberg-Selman levels and stages of moral judgment (or reasoning) are outlined below.

Topical Outline of Levels and Stages in the Development of Moral Judgment

	I.	PRECONVENTIONAL LEVEL
Developmental Stage #1:		Obedience and Punishment Orientation
Developmental Stage #2:		Instrumental Relativistic Orientation
	II.	CONVENTIONAL LEVEL
Developmental Stage #3:		Interpersonal Sharing Orientation

Developmental Stage #4:   Societal Maintenance Orientation

III: PRINCIPLED LEVEL

Developmental Stage #5:   Social-Contract, Human Rights and Welfare Orientation

Developmental Stage #6:   Universal Ethical Principle Orientation

The essential findings and conclusions of the Kohlberg-Selman research team are summarized below.

1. Moral reasoning develops through a series of stages. The researchers studied the same group of individuals over a fifteen-year period and also studied the reasoning of individuals in a number of other cultures (e.g., U.S.A., Taiwan, Malaysian village, Turkey, Mexico, Mayan village). From their findings they concluded that individuals in all parts of the world go through the same sequence of stages in the development of moral reasoning.

2. No stage in moral reasoning can be skipped. The stages are developmental in nature; one stage builds on the previous stage and prepares the individual for the next stage. Thus, it is not possible for a person to jump over a stage, such as moving from stage two directly to stage four.

3. Certain individuals move faster and farther through the stages. There are individual differences in both the rate of moral development and in the highest stage of moral development attained. Kohlberg and Selman found that some individuals take much longer than others to move from a given stage to the next; and they estimate that only about 20 per cent of the adult population ever reach stage five or six of moral reasoning. Most adults operate at stage three or four. An individual can stop (or become "fixated") at any level of moral development.

4. Moral reasoning is related to human behavior.
    The researchers agree that there are many
    factors that influence an individual's moral
    behavior; however, they found that a person's
    stage of moral development was an important
    factor. For example, they found that adoles-
    cents at higher stages of reasoning cheated
    much less often than adolescents at lower
    stages.

5. Moral development is related to the develop-
    ment of a sense of fairness. Kohlberg and
    Selman found that central to a person's think-
    about issues such as truth, duty, sharing,
    or property rights, are the concepts of fair-
    ness and reciprocity. Although young children
    do not think about fairness in terms of
    "rights," they do think about it in terms of
    reciprocity (such as "what's fair for you is
    fair for me").

6. Movement from stage to stage of moral reason-
    ing is a long-term process. The researchers
    were able to observe moral development over
    an extended period of time. They concluded
    that moral development is a long-term process
    for most individuals; there are no sudden
    leaps into higher stages (or levels), but
    rather deliberate progress toward broader,
    more flexible ways of viewing moral problems
    (or dilemmas). Further, they point out that
    the developmental process is not automatic.
    However, they did discover that the process
    could be stimulated by experiences of moral
    conflict, by exchange of different views, and
    by exposure to moral reasoning at a higher
    stage. (The foregoing has tremendous implica-
    tions for education!)

7. Most persons operate rather consistently at a
    given stage. Kohlberg and Selman stress that
    the stages of reasoning are not merely a
    series of possible choices for each individual.
    Actually, each stage can be used as reasoning
    to support yes or no choices on almost any
    question. The same person may use different
    stages at different times (such as using one
    stage when dealing with a value question about
    stealing and another stage when dealing with a

question about the value of life), but usually
individuals are quite consistent. For example,
a person whose predominant stage of reasoning
is stage four will rarely use reasoning at
stages five or three, and will probably never
use reasoning at stages two or six.

Taxonomic Classification

Levels and Stages in the Development of Moral Judgment

I. PRECONVENTIONAL LEVEL

Basis for Moral Judgment: An individual operating
at the Preconventional Level perceives moral value in
external, physical, or quasi-physical happenings, in
bad acts, or in physical or quasi-physical needs rather
than in persons or standards.

At this level, the individual responds to a moral
dilemma in terms of the cultural rules and labels of
good or bad, right or wrong. He interprets the rules
and labels in terms of possible physical or hedonistic
consequences (for instance, punishment, reward, exchange of favors), or in terms of the physical power or
prestige of those whom he identifies with the rules and
labels. This level is divided into developmental
stages 1 and 2.

Developmental Stage #1:	Obedience and Punishment Orientation
Common Characteristics:	These amount to a pre-dominant frame-of-reference (or affective set) which dominate, guide, and focus the individual's thinking when confronted with a moral question (or dilemma).

1. Desire to avoid punishment;

2. Unquestioning obedience to power, prestige,
   authority, and rules;

3. Desire to avoid acts labeled as "bad";

4. Believes that persons who engage in "wrong" acts should be punished;

5. Desires to avoid specific physical damage to persons and to property;

6. Believes that the physical consequences of an act (to persons or to property) determine its "goodness" or "badness" regardless of any other human consideration;

7. Believes that heroes and authorities deserve special treatment or consideration;

8. Inability to relate authority, punishment, rightness, wrongness, and so on, to any underlying social system or moral order.

Developmental Stage #2:   Instrumental Relativistic Orientation

Common Characteristics: These amount to a predominant frame-of-reference (or affective set) which dominate, guide, and focus the individual's thinking when confronted with a moral question (or dilemma).

1. Believes that "right" action is that which instrumentally satisfies the self's needs and sometimes the needs of others (basically a relativistic position from the standpoint of each person's needs or perspective);

2. Interprets human relations and such concepts as fairness, reciprocity, and equal sharing in a market place or physical pragmatic manner (basically a matter of exchanging favors or revenge--"You scratch my back and I'll scratch yours");

3. Believes in concrete rights to property and to individual freedom of choice, regardless of authority;

225

4. Believes in concrete rights of others in the
    sense that "If I have the right, so does the
    other guy."

II. CONVENTIONAL LEVEL

Basis for Moral Judgment: An individual operating
at the Conventional Level perceives moral value in the
performance of good or right roles, in maintaining the
conventional social order, and in the expectancies of
others.

At this level, maintaining, supporting, and conforming to the expectations of the individual's
family, group, or nation is viewed as valuable in its
own right, regardless of the consequences to his own
immediate and obvious needs. The individual is not
only concerned with conformity, but also with the
demonstration of his loyalty through actively supporting and justifying orderliness and stability in the
group. He identifies with the group and its members
and perceives that his moral choices must conform to
the expectations of the group. This level is divided
into developmental stages 3 and 4.

Developmental Stage #3:   Interpersonal Sharing
                            Orientation

Common Characteristics: These amount to a pre-
                            dominant frame-of-refer-
                            ence (or affective set)
                            which dominate, guide,
                            and focus the individu-
                            al's thinking when con-
                            fronted with a moral
                            question (or dilemma).

1. Emphasis on seeking the approval of others
    (thus, good behavior is that which pleases,
    helps, or is expected by others);

2. Emphasis on conforming to stereotyped image
    (or role) and to shared norms of group;

3. Concern for welfare of other group members;

4. Respect for legitimate authority and concern
    with maintaining the accepted rules (or norms);

5. Capable of recognizing and reflecting upon motives and intentions of self and others (the idea of--"He means well" is important).

Developmental Stage #4:   Societal Maintenance Orientation

Common Characteristics: These amount to a pre-dominant frame-of-reference (or affective set) which dominate, guide, and focus the individual's thinking when confronted with a moral question (or dilemma).

1. Accepts society's point of view (and norms); adheres to the moral values and rights associated with society;

2. Concern with helping to maintain the existing stable social system;

3. Respect for duly constituted authority;

4. Emphasis on the individual's duty as a member of society;

5. Believes in necessity of mutual reciprocity between society's point of view and the individual's point of view.

III. PRINCIPLED LEVEL

Basis for Moral Judgment: An individual operating at the Principled Level perceives moral value in conformity of self to shared or shareable standards, rights, duties, or universal principles.

At this level, the individual becomes involved in a conscious effort to identify and clarify moral values and principles which have validity and general applicability apart from the authority of the groups or persons holding the values--and apart from the individual's own identification with such groups or individuals. This level is divided into developmental stages 5 and 6.

Developmental Stage #5:   Social-Contract, Human
                          Rights and Welfare
                          Orientation

Common Characteristics: These amount to a pre-
                          dominant frame-of-refer-
                          ence (or affective set)
                          which dominate, guide,
                          and focus the individu-
                          al's thinking when con-
                          fronted with a moral
                          question (or dilemma).

1. Defines "right" action in terms of individual
    rights and standards that have been examined
    and accepted through societal consensus;

2. Emphasis on the development of procedural
    rules for arriving at societal consensus;

3. Emphasis on a legal point of view, but with
    the built-in possibility of challenging and
    changing the laws in terms of social utility;

4. Belief that in areas beyond what has been
    agreed upon by society, the determination of
    "right" and "wrong" is a matter of personal
    choice by individuals (personal relativism of
    values).

Developmental Stage #6:   Universal Ethical Prin-
                          ciple Orientation

Common Characteristics: These amount to a pre-
                          dominant frame-of-refer-
                          ence (or affective set)
                          which dominate, guide,
                          and focus the individu-
                          al's thinking when con-
                          fronted with a moral
                          question (or dilemma).

1. Defines "right" in terms of consistency with
    self-chosen universal ethical principles of
    (a) respect for human personality (treat each
    as an end, not a means), and (b) respect for
    justice (moral equality of persons);

2. Accepts a universal moral point of view wherein the principles of respect for persons and justice are not tied to any particular culture, but apply to all men everywhere;

3. Employs principles of respect for persons and justice as primary grounds and guide for decisions and duties;

4. Has resolved the problem of ethical relativity and skepticism by appeal to universal principles of human morality (i.e., respect for persons and justice).

Stage Warrants for Harold's Dilemma

In order to assist the teacher in assessing student stage development, a series of sample student responses (position-warrant combinations) is presented below. The responses are intended to be illustrative (rather than exhaustive) of the types of reasoning found at each of the six stages of moral reasoning. In all instances, the position-warrant combinations represent hypothetical reactions to Harold's Dilemma (see Chapter Six).

Stage Warrants	Position A: Harold should tell truth to grand jury	Position B: Harold should lie to grand jury
Stage #1 Warrants	Because anyone who steals (or lies) should be punished.	Because it is always bad to "tattle" on your boss.
	Because the grand jury would be mad if Harold lied to them.	Because Harold's boss would be mad if Harold "squealed" on him.
	Because people should always tell grand juries what they want to know.	Because a kind boss shouldn't have to go to jail with murderers.

Stage Warrants	Position A: Harold should tell truth to grand jury	Position B: Harold should lie to grand jury
Stage #2 Warrants	Because Harold has always paid his taxes and the boss should have to pay his taxes, too. Because being honest and truthful may cause someone to offer Harold an even better job.	Because lots of people lie and get away with it, so Harold can lie and still be friends with his boss. Because Harold might not have a place to work if his boss goes to jail.
Stage #3 Warrants	Because Harold's friends and family would be hurt and unhappy if they found out that Harold lied to the grand jury. Because the boss ought to be stopped before he starts stealing from the employees too, and becomes a worse criminal. Because even though Harold hates to hurt his kind boss, he must tell the truth when the boss hurts the company and the hard-working employees with his stealing and cheating.	Because Harold's fellow employees would no longer be his friends if they knew that he helped to put the boss in jail. Because Harold's fellow employees might be out of work if the boss were to go to jail. Because Harold's boss is really a good man and he probably didn't mean to cheat on his taxes. He won't do it any more!
Stage #4 Warrants	Because we can't allow the breaking of our laws; everyone has a duty to cooperate fully with grand juries.	Because Harold's boss is a public spirited citizen who has made important contributions to our state and nation. He will continue to make such contributions if allowed to run

Stage Warrants	Position A: Harold should tell truth to grand jury	Position B: Harold should lie to grand jury
		his business, rather than "rot" in prison for tax evasion.
	Because Harold's boss should pay his debt to society (by fine or jail), and then get out (or on parole) after learning his lesson and thus, he might be a better person.	Because people all over the country need the product made by the company; if Harold's boss goes to jail the company will probably go out of business and people will have to go without an essential product.
Stage #5 Warrants	Because the grand jury is functioning properly in this instance with respect to the "rights" of both society and the individuals involved (i.e., the grand jury is being fair, has no ulterior motives, and is following proper procedures). After telling the truth, Harold should respectfully request that the jury consider all extenuating circumstances involved in the case, and should also make a plea for mercy for his boss (possible clemency, a fine, or early parole), based on the boss's past record	Because the grand jury is not functioning properly in this instance with respect to the "rights" of both society and the individuals involved (i.e., the grand jury is being unfair, has an "axe" to grind, or is following improper procedures). Although Harold should be willing to accept the legal consequences of lying or refusing to cooperate with the jury, he should make known his intention to work for changes that may overturn the jury's decisions and promote improved grand juries in the future.

Stage Warrants	Position A: Harold should tell truth to grand jury	Position B: Harold should lie to grand jury
	(Perhaps Harold should have tried to get the case settled before going to the grand jury; providing it could have been done in a way consistent with the basic intent of the law and in the best interests of society and the individuals involved.)	(Perhaps Harold should have tried to get the case settled before going to the grand jury; providing it could have been done in a way consistent with the basic intent of the law and in the best interests of society and the individuals involved.)
Stage #6 Warrants	More important than whether or not Harold should tell the truth is the matter of how all of the people involved are to be treated as individual human beings. Those involved in this situation are: the company employees, others in the community and nation, the boss, members of the grand jury, and Harold. If, after careful examination of the issues involved, it appears that telling the truth would help bring about a solution that is fair and ensures respect for the individuality and equality of all concerned, then that is the course Harold should take (with a clear conscience!).	More important than whether or not Harold should tell the truth is the matter of how all of the people involved are to be treated as individual human beings. Those involved in this situation are: the company employees, others in the community and nation, the boss, members of the grand jury, and Harold. If, after careful examination of the issues involved, it appears that lying (or refusal to testify) would help bring about a solution that is fair and ensures respect for the individuality and equality of all concerned, then that is the course Harold should take (with a clear conscience!)

232

Stage Warrants	Position A: Harold should tell truth to grand jury	Position B: Harold should lie to grand jury
	For example, if Harold determines that the boss's motives for tax evasion were purely selfish and destructive of the welfare and individual rights of others, then he should tell the truth to the grand jury (and continue to work for justice and compassion for all concerned).	For example, if Harold determines that the boss's motives for tax evasion were ones that involved non-support for those things that the government has done in violation of the dignity of man, then Harold should lie, or refuse to cooperate with the grand jury, as a means of defending this ethical principle (and continue to work for justice and compassion for all concerned).

[*]Appendix D consists of part of an unpublished paper authored by Charles E. Gray in 1975. See notes 22, 23, 24, and 25 of Chapter Six of this volume.

APPENDIX E

METHODS AND EDUCATIONAL PROGRAMS FOR STIMULATING CREATIVITY: A REPRESENTATIVE LIST

1. <u>Attribute Listing</u>: Emphasizes the detailed obser-
   vation of each particular characteristic or quality
   of an item or situation. Attempts are then made to
   profitably change the characteristic or to relate
   it to a different item. See R. P. Crawford, <u>Direct
   Creativity</u> (with attribute listing) (Wells, Ver-
   mont: Fraser Publishing Company).

2. <u>Awareness Development</u>: A program to increase the
   individual's sensitivity to what is going on within
   himself and how he relates to the here and now.
   See F. S. Perls, R. F. Hefferline, and P. Goodman,
   <u>Gestalt Therapy</u> (New York: Julian Press).

3. <u>Biographical Film Program</u>: An educational program
   of ten documentary biographical films and a flexible textbook. It provides filmed contact with
   exemplary personalities and opportunity to draw
   from students' own inner resources in expressing
   themselves. Designed for college-bound students.
   See Elizabeth M. Drews and D. Knowlton, "The Being
   and Becoming Series for College-Bound Students,"
   <u>Audiovisual Instruction</u>, 8:29-32.

4. <u>Bionics</u>: A technique which seeks discovery in
   nature of ideas which are related to the solution
   of man's problems. For example, attributes of the
   eye of a beetle have suggested new types of ground-
   speed indicators for aircraft. See "Bionics--Part
   II," <u>Professional Engineer and Engineering Digest</u>,
   pp. 16-18.

5. <u>Brainstorming</u>: Promotes rapid and unfettered
   associations in group discussion through defer-
   ment-of-judgment. See A. F. Osborn, <u>Applied
   Imagination</u> (New York: Scribner's).

6. <u>Checklists</u>: Focuses one's attention on a logical
   list of diverse categories to which the problem
   could conceivably relate. See A. F. Osborn,
   <u>Applied Imagination</u> (New York: Scribner's).

7. Creative Analysis: A program of exercises designed to increase the college student's facility in discovering relationships within the knowledge he possesses, and in thereby creating new knowledge. Emphasizes words as tools of the mind and the thought process. Upton and Samson, Creative Analysis (E. P. Dutton and Company, Inc.).

8. Creative Growth Games: Exercises and assists in creative thinking. E. Raudsepp and C. Hough, Creative Growth Games (New York: Harcourt, Brace and World).

9. Creative Thinking Workbook: A program for adults and college-level students; many exercises suitable for high school students. The exercises are designed to remove internal governors and to provide practice in stretching the imagination in problem-finding and problem-solving. Problems are included on product design and on presenting ideas. Can be self-instructional. Available from W. O. Uraneck, 56 Turning Mill Road, Lexington, Massachusetts 02173. (Uraneck also published 101 Cases--Creative Problem Solving.)

10. Forced Relationship Techniques: Specific types of exercises designed to derive new combinations of items and thoughts. See C. S. Whiting, Creative Thinking (New York: Reinhold Publishing Corporation).

11. General Semantics: Approaches which help the individual to discover multiple meanings or relationships in words and expressions. See S. I. Hayakawa, Language in Thought and Action (New York: Harcourt, Brace and World, Inc.). For continuing current information, see ETC: A Review of General Semantics, a quarterly journal with editorial offices at San Francisco State College, San Francisco, California 94132. (Business office: 540 Powell Street, San Francisco, California 94108.)

12. Incident Process: A problem-solving approach (and/or training program) developed at the college and adult level. It stresses multiple viewpoints and a wide search for problem-elements; applies many methods similar to the older Job Relations Training program. See P. W. Pigors and F. C. Pigors, Case Method in Human Relations: The

236

Incident *Process* (New York: McGraw-Hill Book Company, Inc.).

13. *Kepner-Tregoe* *Method*: An approach (or training program) that emphasizes "what a man does with information," i.e., how he interrelates facts in analyzing problems and making decisions. Developed at adult level. See C. H. Kepner and B. B. Tregoe, *The* *Rational* *Manager* (New York: McGraw-Hill Book Company, Inc.)

14. *Morphology* (*or* *Morphological* *Analysis*): A system involving the methodical interrelating of all elements of a problem in order to discover new approaches to a solution. See M. S. Allen, *Morphological* *Creativity* (Englewood Cliffs, New Jersey: Prentice-Hall, Inc.).

15. *Problem-Solving* *Training*: A program on problem-solving skills for high-IQ first graders. Consists of units called "games." Presented by the teacher as a programmed script for individual instruction (one child at a time). See R. C. Anderson, "Can First Graders Learn an Advanced Problem-Solving Skill?", *Journal* *of* *Educational* *Psychology*, 56(6):283-94.

16. *Productive-Divergent* *Thinking* *Model*: An approach designed to help elementary teachers integrate the teaching of factors such as fluency, flexibility, originality, and so on, with the teaching of subject matter. Contact Director, Creativity and National Schools Projects, Macalester College, Saint Paul, Minnesota 55101.

17. *Productive* *Thinking* *Program*: A self-instructional program for the upper grades of elementary school. It attempts to increase the number of elements that are taken into consideration in problem solving. Available from Educational Innovation, Box 9248, Berkeley, California 94719. See R. M. Olton, "A Self-Instructional Program for the Development of Productive Thinking in Fifth and Sixth Grade Children," in First Seminar on *Productive* *Thinking* *in* *Education*, ed. F. E. Williams (St. Paul, Minnesota: Creativity and National Schools Project, Macalester College).

18. Psychodramatic Approaches: These include a
    variety of techniques such as role playing and
    role reversal. In psychodrama the attempt is
    made to bring into focus all elements of an indi-
    vidual's problem; whereas in sociodrama the
    emphasis is on shared problems of group members.
    Elements of these techniques have been used in
    various types of educational settings and train-
    ing programs. See J. L. Moreno, Who Shall Sur-
    vive? (New York: Beacon House). For current
    reading, see the quarterly journal Group Psycho-
    therapy by the same publisher.

19. Self-Enhancing Education: Emphasis on basic
    principles of creative problem-solving, including
    education for setting as well as solving one's
    own problems. See Norma Randolph and W. A. Howe,
    Self-Enhancing Education, A Program to Motivate
    Learners (Palo Alto, California: Sanford Press;
    Sanford Office, 200 California Avenue, Palo Alto,
    California).

20. Self-Instructional Course in Applied Imagination:
    A programmed set of twenty-eight self-instruc-
    tional booklets. See "Programming Creative Be-
    havior," Research Project No. 5-0716, Contractual
    No. OE-7-42-1630-314, Educational Research Infor-
    mation Center, Room 3-0-083, 400 Maryland Avenue,
    S.W., Washington, D.C. 20202.

21. Synectics (or Operational Creativity): A training
    program which stresses the practical use of
    analogy and metaphor in problem solving. The
    Synectics mechanisms "force new ideas and associ-
    ations up for conscious consideration rather than
    waiting for them to arise fortuitously." Devel-
    oped at adult level. See W. J. J. Gordon,
    Synectics (New York: Harper and Row Publishers).
    For current information about this training pro-
    gram, write Synectics, Inc., 28 Church Street,
    Cambridge, Massachusetts 02138.

22. Torrance Programmed Experiences: Exercise books,
    recorded exercises including "sounds and images,"
    and biographical recordings about creative
    people. These provide example, stimulus, and
    opportunity for making fresh, imaginative associ-
    ations. Developed at elementary school level;
    sounds and images available at adult level

also. Available as <u>Ideabooks</u> by R. E. Myers and
E. P. Torrance; and <u>Imagi/Craft</u> <u>Series</u> <u>in</u> <u>Creative</u>
<u>Development</u> by B. F. Cunnington and E. P.
Torrance (Boston: Ginn and Company). See E. P.
Torrance and R. Gupta, "Development and Evalua-
tion of Recorded Programmed Experiences in
Creative Thinking in the Fourth Grade," a re-
search project performed under the provisions of
Title VII of the National Defense Act of 1958
(P. L. 85-864) with the New Educational Media
Branch, U.S. Office of Education, Department of
Health, Education, and Welfare.

23. <u>Value</u> <u>Engineering</u> (<u>or</u> <u>Value</u> <u>Analysis</u>, <u>Value</u> <u>Inno-</u>
<u>vation</u>, <u>Value</u> <u>Management</u>, <u>and</u> <u>so</u> <u>on</u>): Training
programs applying general principles of creative
problem-solving to group efforts toward reducing
costs or optimizing value. Adult level. See
L. D. Miles, <u>Techniques</u> <u>of</u> <u>Value</u> <u>Analysis</u> <u>and</u>
<u>Engineering</u> (New York: McGraw-Hill Book Company,
Inc.); also <u>Value</u> <u>Engineering</u> Handbook, H111, U.S.
Department of Defense (U.S. Government Printing
Office, Washington, D.C.). For current informa-
tion, conference reports, bibliographies, and so
on, write Society of American Value Engineers,
Windy Hill, Suite E-9, 1741 Roswell Street,
Smyrna, Georgia 30080.

24. WFF'N PROOF: A symbolic logic game designed to
increase one's ability to discover new relationships in a logical manner. Portions applicable
at elementary level, proceeding through adult
levels. Available from author, L. E. Allen
(<u>WFF'N</u> <u>PROOF</u>, <u>The</u> <u>Game</u> <u>of</u> <u>Modern</u> <u>Logic</u>), P.O.
Box 71, New Haven, Connecticut 06501.

25. <u>Work</u> <u>Simplification</u>: An industrial training program that applies some of the general principles
of creative problem-solving to the simplification
of operations or procedures. Provides opportunity for personnel to use their mental resources
in helping improve organizational operations,
using simple industrial engineering principles.
("Job Methods Training," as well as other similarly named programs of World War II and thereafter,
applied the basic concepts of this program.)
See H. F. Goodwin, "Work Simplification" (a documentary series of articles), <u>Factory</u> <u>Management</u>
<u>and</u> <u>Maintenance</u>. Briefer but more recent

information may be obtained from Work Simplification Conferences, P.O. Box 30, Lake Placid, New York 12947.

26. <u>Young</u> <u>Thinkers</u>: For children between five and ten years of age. A series of more than fifty projects and exercises which can be used by the individual or by groups. These have been used in the home and in schools. Available from W. O. Uraneck, 56 Turning Mill Road, Lexington, Massachusetts 02173.

INDEX

Activating (Level 2), 68-70
  deliberate modeling, 70
  mimicry, 69-70
  physical outputs, 68-70
Affect
  defined, 101-02
Affective action poten-
  tial, 22-23, 49-50
Affective behaviors, 33
Affective Classification
  Model (Pierce-Gray),
  45-59
  Affective Creating
    (Level 6), 56-58
  Affective Judging (Level
    5), 55-56
  Affective Perceiving
    (Level 1), 48-49
  Conforming (Level 3),
    52-53
  Reacting (Level 2), 49-
    52
  summary of levels of the
    affective domain, 59,
    201
  Validating (Level 4),
    53-54
Affective clichés, 189
Affecting Creating (Level
  6), 56-58
  inspirational insight,
    57-58
  integrating values, 57

Affective development
  cultural crises, 36
  developmental tendencies,
    35-36
  in changing society, 36
  in static society, 35-36
  self concept, 35
Affective domain
  classification model,
    201
  vagueness of, 7
Affective domain taxonomy
  (Krathwohl), 42-44
  characterization, 44
  organization, 43-44
  receiving, 43
  responding, 43
  valuing, 43
Affective education
  contemporary approaches
    to, 34
  historical approaches to,
    34
Affective goals
  behavioral, 103, 115-16
  procedural, 103, 115-16
  substantive, 103, 115-16
Affective Judging (Level
  5), 55-56
  establishing value cri-
    teria, 55-56
  value judging, 56

Affective objectives
    examples of, 113-16
    guidelines for, 109-13
Affective Perceiving
        (Level 1), 48-49
    emotive imprinting, 49
    response setting, 49
Affective teaching strate-
        gies
    activating creative
        imagination, 158-59
    moral reasoning defined,
        118
    moral reasoning strate-
        gies, 147-58
    types of strategies, 117
    value analysis defined,
        117-18
    value analysis strate-
        gies, 138-47
    value clarification de-
        fined, 117
    value clarification
        strategies, 118-38
Alcorn, Marvin, 197
Allen, George H., 182
Analyzing (Level 4), 26-27
    comparative analysis, 27
    logical analysis, 27
Applying (Level 3), 25-26
    complex application, 26
    routine application, 25
    procedural application,
        25-26
Arici, H., 98
Aristotle
    growth impulse, 2
Attitudes
    defined, 102-03
Authentic problems ap-
        proach, 125-28

Behavioral goals, 103
Binet, Alfred
    performance test scales,
        14-15
Bloom, B. S.
    categories of human be-
        havior; 3-4

cognitive taxonomy, 20
taxonomies, 12
Taxonomy of Educational
    Objectives: Cogni-
    tive Domain, 32
Bowyer, Carlton H., 11
Brady, Marion
    cultural value system
        approach, 134-36
    "The Key Concept," 161
Brain hemispheres, 48, 196
Brainstorming, 97-98
Broudy, Harry S.
    Building a Philosophy of
        Education, 61
    intrinsic and instrumen-
        tal valuing, 41-42
Brown, G. I., 182
Bruner, Jerome, 32

Cardinal principles of
    education, 11
Central purpose of Ameri-
    can education, 11
Chadwick, James
    "procedures for value
        analysis," 161
    value analysis model,
        139-41
Cherry, Clare, 181
Clarifying response ap-
    proach, 129-34
Classification model for
    the cognitive, affec-
    tive, and psychomotor
    domains, 201
Classifying objectives
    assumptions about, 9
Cognitive action potential,
    22-23
Cognitive Classification
    Model (Pierce-Gray),
    21-30
    Analyzing (Level 4), 26-
        27
    Applying (Level 3), 25-
        26
    Cognitive Creating (Level
        6), 29-30

242

Cognitive Judging (Level
    5), 27-29
Cognitive Perceiving
    (Level 1), 21-24
Understanding (Level 2),
    24-25
Cognitive clichés, 189
Cognitive Creating (Level
    6), 29-30
Creative Insight, 30
Uniting Ideas, 29
Cognitive domain
    abilities of, 4
    classification model, 201
    defined, 3-4
    emphasis of, 3-6
    popularity of, 4-5
Cognitive domain taxonomy
    (Bloom), 20
Cognitive Judging (Level
    5), 27-29
Establishing Ideational
    Criteria, 28
Ideational Judging, 29
Cognitive objectives, 80-
    83
Cognitive Perceiving
    (Level 1), 21-24
Focusing, 23
Storing, 24
Cognitive teaching strate-
    gies, 84-98
discussions, 94
exposition, 84-86
inquiry learning, 90-94
interaction techniques,
    88-90
self-instructional
    materials, 86-88
to inspire creativity,
    94-98, 235-40
Committee on Secondary
    School Studies, 11
Computer-assisted instruc-
    tion, 86-87
Conforming (Level 3), 52-
    53
artificial attitude, 52-
    53

consistent attitude, 53
rationalized attitude,
    53
Coombs, Jerrold
    teaching strategies for
        value analysis, 161
    value analysis model,
        139-41
Cox, C. Benjamin
    defensible partisanship,
        104-05
    Inquiry in Social
        Studies, 160
Cratty, B. J., 181, 182
Creative imagination
    strategies for activat-
        ing, 158-59, 235
Creativity, 94-98
    brainstorming, 97-98
    stimulating, 94-96, 235-
        40
Cultural value system ap-
    proach, 134-36, 203-
    07

Debates, 90
Deciphering the learning
    domains, 201
Defensible partisanship,
    104-05
Demonstrations, 84-85
Descartes
    involuntary behavior, 13
    mind-body dualism, 2
    voluntary behavior, 13
Development of moral judg-
    ment, 221-33
Discovery learning, 89-90
Discussions, 94
Domain balance
    in bullfighting, 192-93
    in hypothetical secondary
        school, 193-96
    in schools, 193
    shifts in emphasis, 190-
        93
    struggles for, 188-90
Domain CAP, 183-85

Douglass, H. R., 11

Early childhood education,
168
Eberhard, V., 181
Educational Policies Com-
mission, 11
Egstrom, G., 181
Emotions, 49-50
distress and delight, 49
Empathetic approach, 136-
38
Etheridge, G. W., 32
Executing (Level 3), 70-71
operational execution,
70-71
skilled execution, 71
task execution, 70
Exposition, 84-86
demonstrations, 84-85
instructional media,
85-86
lecture, 84

Fenton, Edwin, 160, 163
Fleishman, E. A., 182
Fraenkel, Jack R.
Helping Students Think
and Value, 160
value inference approach,
26-28
Friedman, S. J., 181

Gagné, Robert
"Analysis of Instruction-
al Objectives and the
Design of Instruction,"
32
seven forms of learning,
18-20
Getz, Howard G., 98
Gordon, William J. J., 61
Synectics, 159, 163
Gray, Charles E.
authentic problems ap-
proach, 125-28, 160

cultural value system
approach, 134-36,
203-07
Heuristic Evaluative
Model, 144-47, 209-
20, 161-62
Teaching Model for Moral
Reasoning, 152-58,
221-33, 162
Value Education Out-
comes, 60
Guilford, J. P.
contents dimension, 16
Nature of Human Intelli-
gence, 11, 32, 196
operations and content,
3-4
operations dimension, 16-
17
products dimension, 17
Structures of Intellect
(SOI) model, 16-18
Guthrie, E. R., 14

Hallman, Ralph J., 98
Harrow, A. J.
psychomotor classifica-
tion model, 65-66
Taxonomy of Psychomotor
Domain, 75-76
"standard model," 69
Hauenstein, A. D.
Curriculum Planning for
Behavioral Develop-
ment, 75
psychomotor classifica-
tion model, 65
Hebb, D. O., 181
Heuristic Evaluative Model,
144-47, 209-20
Hierarchy of needs of man
(Maslow), 39-41
aesthetic, 41
belongingness, 40-41
esteem, 41
knowledge and understand-
ing, 41
physiological, 39-40

safety, 40
self-actualization, 41
Holding, D. H., 182
Hull, C. L., 14
Hunt, Maurice P.
  authentic problems ap-
    proach, 125-28
  Teaching High School
    Social Studies, 160

Ideomotor training, 172-73
Imperative needs of youth
  of secondary school
  age, 11
Inquiry learning, 90-94
Instructional media, 85-86
Interaction techniques,
  88-90
  discovery learning, 89-
    90
  panels, reports, and de-
    bate, 90
  simulations and games,
    89
Intrinsic and instrumental
  valuing (Broudy), 41-
    42
  appetitive principle,
    41-42
  conflicts between desire,
    want, and need, 42

Jones, W. T., 11
Jurisprudential approach,
  142-43

Kibler, R. J.
  Behavioral Objectives and
    Instruction, 75, 182
  psychomotor classifica-
    tion model, 64-65
Kohlberg, Lawrence
  levels of moral judgment,
    148-52, 162-63, 197
Konicek, R. D., 197

Krathwohl, David R.
  affective domain taxon-
    omy, 42-44
  Taxonomy of Educational
    Objectives: Affec-
    tive Domain, 61
  Taxonomy of Educational
    Objectives: Cogni-
    tive Domain, 12

Learning principles
  individualizing instruc-
    tion, 176
  knowledge of results,
    175-76
  perceived purpose, 175
  revelation of objectives,
    174-75
Lecky, Prescott, 60
Lecture, 84
Lindgren, H. C., 99
Linear reading programs, 87
Ludwig, D. H., 182

Maneuvering (Level 4), 71-
    72
  Inspecting Skills, 71-72
  Selecting Skills, 72
Maslow, Abraham
  hierarchy of needs of
    man, 39-41, 60
Massialas, B. G.
  defensible partisanship,
    104-05
  Inquiry in Social Studies,
    160
Meadow, A., 99
Metcalf, L. E.
  authentic problems ap-
    proach, 125-28
  Teaching High School
    Social Studies, 60,
    160
  value analysis, 139
  Value Education: Ratio-
    nale, Strategies, and
    Procedures, 161

Methods and educational
programs for stimu-
lating creativity,
235-40
Meux, Milton
procedures for value
analysis, 161
teaching strategies for
value analysis, 161
value analysis model,
139-41
Model for the analysis and
comparison of cultural
value systems, 203-07
Moment of meaning, 21-22,
48
Money, John, 181
Moore, R. S., 181
Moral dilemma, 148-49,
152-54, 221-33
Moral judgment
and educational practice,
151-52
conventional level, 149-
50
pre-conventional level,
149
principled level, 150
Moral reasoning
and value conflict, 148-
49
defined, 118
dilemmas, 148-49, 152-
54, 221-33
levels of, 149-50
strategies, 147-58, 221-
33
Moral reasoning strategies
and levels of moral
judgment, 149-50
and value conflicts,
148-49
purposes of, 147-48
teaching model for moral
reasoning, 152-58,
221-33

National Education Association Committee on
College Entrance Re-
quirements, 11
Nevin, John A., 31
Newmann, Fred M.
Clarifying Public Con-
troversy, 161
jurisprudential approach,
142-43

Objectives
affective examples, 113-
16
assumptions about, 9
cognitive examples, 80-
83
for public education, 1
psychomotor examples,
167-80
Ogburn, W. F., 60
Ogden, C. K., 21-22
Meaning of Meaning, 32
Oliver, Donald W.
jurisprudential approach,
142-43
Taking a Stand, 161
Teaching Public Issues in
the High School, 161
Osborn, A. F., 61

Panels, 90
Parnes, Sidney J., 98-99
Physical action potential,
67-68
Pierce, Walter D.
"Relationships Among
Teaching, Cognitive
Levels, Testing, and
IQ," 98
Pierce-Gray Classification
Model for the Affec-
tive Domain, 45-59
Affective Creating (Level
1), 56-58

Affective Judging (Level 5), 55-56
Affective Perceiving (Level 1), 48-49
brain hemispheres, 48
cognitive-affective continuum, 47
Conforming (Level 3), 52-53
degree of cognition, 46-47
Reacting (Level 2), 49-52
sorting factors, 45-47
summary of levels of the affective domain, 59, 201
Validating (Level 4), 53-54
Pierce-Gray Classification Model for the Cognitive, Affective, and Psychomotor Domains, 201
Pierce-Gray Classification Model for the Cognitive Domain, 21-31
Analyzing (Level 4), 26-27
Applying (Level 3), 25-26
assumptions, 21
basic intellectual skill, 21
Cognitive Creating (Level 6), 29-30
Cognitive Judging (Level 5), 27-29
Cognitive Perceiving (Level 1), 21-24
summary of levels in the cognitive domain, 30-31, 201
Understanding (Level 2), 24-25
Pierce-Gray Classification Model for the Psychomotor Domain, 66-75

Activating (Level 2), 68-70
Executing (Level 3), 70-71
Maneuvering (Level 4), 71-72
Psychomotor Creating (Level 6), 73-74
Psychomotor Judging (Level 5), 72-73
Psychomotor Perceiving (Level 1), 67-68
summary of levels in the psychomotor domain, 74-75, 201
Planning
affective objectives, activities, and evaluations in affective domain, 105-08, 108-16
cognitive domain, 80-83
cognitive objectives, activities, and evaluations, 77-79
psychomotor objectives, activities, and evaluations, 165-66
psychomotor domain, 167
to ensure cross-section of cognitive levels, 79-80
Popham, James, 182
Procedural goals, 103
Process of valuing (Raths), 37-39
acting, 37-38
choosing, 37-38
prizing, 37-38
value indicators, 38
Psychomotor action potential, 22-23
Psychomotor activating strategies, 168-73
Psychomotor Classification Model (Pierce-Gray), 67-74
Activating (Level 2), 68-70

Executing (Level 3), 70-71
Maneuvering (Level 4), 71-72
Psychomotor Creating (Level 6), 73-74
Psychomotor Judging (Level 5), 72-73
Psychomotor Perceiving (Level 1), 67-68
summary of levels in the psychomotor domain, 74-75, 201
Psychomotor classification models
Harrow model, 65-66
Hauenstein model, 65
Kibler model, 64-65
Pierce-Gray model, 66-75, 201
problems with models, 66
Ragsdale model, 63-64
Simpson model, 64
Psychomotor clichés, 189
Psychomotor Creating (Level 6), 73-74
combining skills, 73-74
performance insight, 74
Psychomotor creating strategies, 178-80
Psychomotor development
cephalocaudal principle, 68
motor chaining, 68
proximodistal principle, 68
Psychomotor domain
classification model, 201
ignored, 8
Psychomotor domain taxonomy (Harrow), 65-66
Psychomotor executing strategies, 173-76
Psychomotor Judging (Level 5), 72-73
Establishing Performance Criteria, 73

Performance Judging, 73
Psychomotor judging strategies, 178
Psychomotor maneuvering strategies, 176-78
Psychomotor objectives
characteristics of, 165-66
neglect of higher levels, 166
revelation of, 174-75
Psychomotor Perceiving (Level 1), 67-68
physiofunctional maintenance, 67-68
sensory transmission, 67
Psychomotor perceiving strategies, 168-71
Psychomotor teaching strategies
activating strategies, 168-73
creating strategies, 178-80
deliberate modeling strategies, 172-73
executing strategies, 173-76
judging strategies, 178
maneuvering strategies, 176-78
perceiving strategies, 168-71

Ragsdale, C. E.
"How Children Learn Motor Types of Activities," 75
psychomotor relationships, 63-64
Raths, Louis E.
clarifying response approach, 129-34
process of valuing model, 37-39
value sheet approach, 120-22

Values and Teaching, 60, 160
Reacting (Level 2), 49-52
  controlling, 52-53
  emoting, 50-51
  recognizing, 51-52
Readings, 86
Relationship between domains
  at Level 1, 185
  at Level 2, 186
  at Level 3, 186
  at Level 4, 187
  at Level 5, 187
  at Level 6, 187-88
  Domain CAP, 183-85
Reports, 90
Rest, James, 163
Richards, I. A., 22
  Meaning of Meaning, 32
Runnels, Max R., 197

Self-instructional materials
  computer-assisted instruction, 86-87
  linear reading programs, 87
  readings, 86
  self-instructional packages, 87-88
Self-instructional packages, 87-88
Shaver, James P.
  jurisprudential approach, 142-43
  Teaching Public Issues in the High School, 161
Simon, Sidney B.
  value priority approach, 122-23
  "Values-Clarification vs. Indoctrination," 160
Simpson, E. J.
  Classification of Educational Objectives: Psychomotor Domain, 75

psychomotor classification model, 64
Simulations and games, 89
Skinner, B. F., 14
Small, George, 182
Spearman, C.
  Abilities of Man, 31
  "g" and "s" factors, 15
Specific language disability
  characteristics of, 169-71
Stebbins, R. J., 182
Structure of Intellect (SOI) model, 17, 37
Stuart, Marion F.
  Neurophysiological Insight into Teaching, 181
  specific language disability, 169-71
Substantive goals, 103
Synectics, 159

Taba, Hilda, 161
Taxonomies of psychomotor domain
  critique of, 9
Taxonomy of affective domain
  critique of, 7-8
Taxonomy of cognitive domain
  categories, 3-4
Teacher role
  in affective domain, 104-05
Teaching Model for Moral Reasoning, 147-58, 221-33
Thorndike, E. L.
  animal intelligence, 31
  constellations of abilities, 2
  law of effect, 14-15
Thurstone, L. L.
  primary factors, 15

"Primary Mental Abilities Scale," 31
Tolman, E. C., 14
Tracy, William, 197

Understanding (Level 2), 24-25
  conceptualizing, 24-25
  rendering, 24
  retrieving, 24
Upton, Albert W.
  categories of human behavior, 2-3
  category system, 15-16
  classification, 16
  Design for Thinking, 12, 32
  on meaning, 21-22
  operational analysis, 16
  structural analysis, 16

Validating (Level 4), 53-54
Value analysis
  defined, 117-18
  model, 139-41
  strategies, 138-47
Value analysis model, 139-41
Value analysis strategies
  Heuristic Evaluative Model, 144-47, 209-20
  jurisprudential approach, 142-43
  objectives for, 139
  purpose of, 138-39
  value analysis model, 139-41

Value clarification
  defined, 117
  limitations, 134, 138
  strategies, 118-38
Value clarification strategies
  authentic problems approach, 125-28
  clarifying response approach, 129-34
  cultural value system approach, 134-36
  empathetic approach, 136-38
  frames-of-reference, 119-20
  purpose of, 118-19
  value inference approach, 123-24
  value priority approach, 122-23
  value sheet approach, 120-22
Value conflicts
  in changing society, 35-36
  value inference approach, 123-24
  value priority approach, 122-23
  value sheet approach, 120-22
Values
  defined, 102-03
  moral reasoning, 118
  value analysis, 117-18
  value clarification, 117
Vanek, M., 182